The Archetypal Imagination

NUMBER EIGHT
Carolyn and Ernest Fay Series in Analytical Psychology
David H. Rosen, General Editor

The Archetypal Imagination

JAMES HOLLIS

Foreword by David H. Rosen

TEXAS A&M UNIVERSITY PRESS
College Station

The paper used in this book
meets the minimum requirements
of the American National Standard for Permanence
of Paper for Printed Library Materials, z39.48-1984.
Binding materials have been
chosen for durability.

For a complete list of books in print in this series,
see the back of the book.

Library of Congress Cataloging-in-Publication Data

Hollis, James, 1940–
    The archetypal imagination / James Hollis ;
foreword by David H. Rosen. — 1st ed.
        p.   cm. — (Carolyn and Ernest Fay series
in analytical psychology ; no. 8)
        Includes bibliographical references and index.
        ISBN 0-89096-932-9 (cloth : alk. paper);
        ISBN 1-58544-268-2 (pbk.)
        1. Archetype (Psychology)   2. Imagination
3. Jungian psychology.   4. Psychoanalysis.
I. Title.   II. Series.
BF175.5.A72H65   2000
153.3—dc21   99-057388
                                        CIP

NUMBER EIGHT
Carolyn and Ernest Fay Series in Analytical Psychology
David H. Rosen, General Editor

The Carolyn and Ernest Fay edited book series, based initially on the annual Fay Lecture Series in Analytical Psychology, was established to further the ideas of C. G. Jung among students, faculty, therapists, and other citizens and to enhance scholarly activities related to analytical psychology. The Book Series and Lecture Series address topics of importance to the individual and to society. Both series were generously endowed by Carolyn Grant Fay, the founding president of the C. G. Jung Educational Center in Houston, Texas. The series are in part a memorial to her late husband, Ernest Bel Fay. Carolyn Fay has planted a Jungian tree carrying both her name and that of her late husband, which will bear fruitful ideas and stimulate creative works from this time forward. Texas A&M University and all those who come in contact with the growing Fay Jungian tree are extremely grateful to Carolyn Grant Fay for what she has done. The holder of the McMillan Professorship in Analytical Psychology at Texas A&M functions as the general editor of the Fay Book Series.

Contents

Illustrations

Foreword

Imagination is more important than information.

—Albert Einstein

This book on archetypal imagination is critically needed medicine in this world where information engulfs us. It also serves as a dose of imaginative soul to help immunize us against the overwhelming expansion of ego-based information technology. In addition to writing this book, James Hollis has done us a great service by emphasizing in it the universal and ancient roots of imagination, which represent a kind of natural health food available to us, at all times, from within. Hollis challenges us to follow Anthony Storr's prescription from *Solitude: A Return to the Self* because it fuels the creative imagination and its spiritual, artistic, and therapeutic manifestations.[1] As Joan Chodorow has written, "Jung's analytic method is based upon the [innate] healing function of the imagination."[2] Jung's concept of active imagination (the same thing as creative imagination) requires a meditative state in which the ego is relaxed. This state of reverie allows access to the vast inner world of ancient, but living, symbols. Once in this state, a person can utilize *wu wei* (the Taoist concept of "creative quietude") in order to begin the process of letting things happen in the psyche, which culminates in a creative product or work of art.[3]

Imagination is the eye of the soul.

—Joseph Joubert

Being alone (all One) with nature is intricately tied to human imagination and the divine, which is the focus of chapter 1, "Religious Imaginings." Hollis amplifies Jung's central archetype of the Self—the numinous Mystery—which is often experienced as inner or outer light in the abyss of darkness. The archetypal and instinctual soul image is at the core of all religious experiences that transform a life of neurotic suffering into one of hope and meaning. Over and over Hollis reveals how healing and wisdom (that is, spiritual knowledge) occur, and he shows how these are related to symbols of transformation and creative, active imagination.

> *An uncommon degree of imagination*
> *constitutes poetical genius.*
> —Dugald Stewart

In chapter 2, "Literary Imaginings," Hollis utilizes two of Rainer Maria Rilke's poems from the *Duino Elegies* to illustrate how words create numinous images that provide divine inspiration and celebrate the awesome mystery of life, love, and death. Rilke writes creatively about all things ordinary and extraordinary. Hollis underscores Rilke's healing message to "praise this world to the angel." Rilke knew that the spiritual realm alone is the source of ultimate meaning, and his discovery of that truth lives on through his poetry.

> *Everything you can imagine is real.*
> —Pablo Picasso

In chapter 3, "Incarnational Imaginings," Hollis leads us to an understanding of the painter's view of eternity. Hollis singles out Nancy Witt, a contemporary artist whose brilliant and imaginative work depicts a visionary world. Through Hollis's descriptions, we view the active imagination process of a gifted artist. It is clear that Witt taps into the collective unconscious and our common spiritual heritage. We see and learn about her growth and development, and we are stimulated to develop pictures of our own lives and myths and of what lies beyond our coming deaths.

The lunatic, the lover, and the poet, are
of imagination all compact.

—William Shakespeare

Shakespeare knew, as did Plato, that love and poetry are kinds of madness all tied to soulful imagination. It follows that psychotherapy and soul are "Therapeutic Imaginings," the subject of Hollis's fourth chapter. One of Jung's greatest gifts was to treasure the creative aspects of mental illness. As Jung did, Hollis emphasizes that the creative spark of soul, in the troubled imagination of the psychologically and psychiatrically disturbed, contains healing qualities leading to recovery and renewal of purpose and meaning. As Hollis carefully outlines, the soul has left modern psychology and psychiatry, and it must be retrieved and rekindled before individual and collective healing can occur. Much of chapter 4 concerns the creative, soulful, and healing doctor-patient relationship. The wounded healer knows how to engage the patient's problem, honor sacred dreams, and activate imagination and creativity, which all help the wounded patient heal. An encouraging development in psychology and psychiatry is evident by the recent focus on joy, inspiration, and hope and caring for the psyche or soul and its unique, creative, and evolutionary nature.[4]

Alice Walker has said:

Our shame is deep. For shame is the result of soul injury. Mirrors, however, are sacred, not only because they permit us to witness the body we are fortunate this time around to be in, but because they permit us to ascertain the condition of the eternal that rests behind the body, the soul. As an ancient Japanese proverb states: when the mirror is dim, the soul is not pure.

Art is the mirror, perhaps the only one, in which we can see our true collective face. We must honor its sacred function. We must let art help us.[5]

In response to Walker's profoundly true reflection of our condition, Hollis shows us that the archetypal imagination is the way to spiritual re-awakening, creative products (that is, art), and soulful healing. This book is a lovely and timely gift.

David H. Rosen
College Station, Texas

Acknowledgments

I was asked to deliver the Fay Lectures at Texas A&M University long before the prospect of living in Texas ever occurred to me. Since moving to Texas in 1998 and becoming director of the C. G. Jung Educational Center of Houston, I have gained David Rosen and Carolyn Grant Fay as friends and colleagues. Carolyn's vision and generosity in creating and sustaining the beautiful Jung Center of Houston for over four decades, and the Fay Lecture and Book Series in Analytical Psychology, have been wondrous gifts of Jung to several generations past and many more to come. To both I am grateful for the invitation to speak at the distinguished Fay Lectures, as I have enormous respect for those who have spoken before me.

This book is dedicated to Jill, to our children, Taryn and Timothy, Jonah and Seah, our grandchildren Rachel and Nicholas, and to the people of the Jung Educational Center of Houston with whom I am privileged to work. I also wish to thank artist Nancy Witt for allowing me to discuss her work, reproduced here in photographs courtesy of Katherine Wetzel. And may I also thank Maureen Creamer Bemko for her deft editing. Any book, even one written by a solitary, is the work of many.

The Archetypal Imagination

Archetypal Imaginings

The Golden String Which Leads to Heaven's Gate

What we wish most to know, most desire, remains unknowable and lies beyond our grasp. Each of the chapters that follow begins with this same sentence, a reminder of the central dilemma of our condition—the *Sehnsucht für Ewigekeit* or yearning for eternity, as the Romantics defined it—and our existential limitations, finitude, and impotence before the immensity of the cosmos. Our endeavor here will be heuristic. It will not solve any problem, for the human dilemma is insoluble, but it may allow us to appreciate more deeply the yearning which we embody, and the resources which we have employed to mediate the unfathomable abyss between longing and connection. In a letter the nineteenth-century novelist Gustave Flaubert succinctly expressed this paradox: "Human speech is like a cracked kettle on which we tap crude rhythms for bears to dance to, while we long to make music that would melt the stars." Such images as cracked kettles and dancing bears hardly ennoble humans, but the juxtaposition with the distant longing, which the stars suggest, certainly creates an affective bridge across that abyss which we all experience. Or we think of Thomas Nashe, in his effort to conjure with the inexplicable horrors of a sixteenth-century outbreak of the Black Death in his "A Litany in Time of Plague."

> *Brightness falls from the air.*
> *Queens have died, young and fair.*
> *Dust hath closed Helen's eye.*[1]

It is not so much that death shocks or surprises us, Nashe suggests, but that there are, finally, no exceptions, no exemptions. As Job found to his dismay, we have no signed contract with the Party of the First Part, and all things fall. Brightness itself falls. Even queens, young and comely, are no exception. We are reminded by the death of Britain's Princess Diana that the queenly may die as easily in a squalid Parisian tunnel as in state. But the movement of the images from the abstract brightness to the more particular queens to the individual Helen reminds us of the equality of mortality, the democracy of dust. Here again, the utilization of imaginative figures helps us cross the bridge from the knowable world to the unknowable, just as dreams help us intimate a relationship with that which, categorically, we can never know: the presence and intention of the unconscious.

The thoughts now transformed into the chapters of this book were influenced by the metaphors and inquiring spirits of two imaginative sensibilities: Jung and Blake. Both were intuitives with a keen eye for the suggestive detail, the reading of the surface to intimate the implicit subtext or the layers of meaning which are embodied through the image but which are indiscernible to the sensate eye. Just as any good therapist is obliged to read the surface of presentations and discern the hidden motives, the wounded permutations of eros, and the implicit strategies of healing, so the spiritually sensitive person remembers, in the words of the Surrealist poet Paul Éluard, "There is another world, and it is this one."

Humankind has developed resources to intimate the unfathomable, to help us reach for the hem of the gods and goddesses, and to stand in the presence of infinite values. We call these resources *metaphor* (something that will "carry over" from one thing to another) and *symbol* (something that will "project toward" convergence). With metaphor and symbol, we are provisionally able to approximate, to apprehend, to appreciate that which lies beyond our powers to understand or to control. Unfortunately, our species is prone to fall in love with its own creations and to reify them, converting them from intimations to concepts. By encapsulating the mystery, we lose it entirely. This is the terrible temptation of literalist fundamentalism of all kinds. When the temptation triumphs, the images that arise out of primal experience, phenomenological in character, are subordinated to the needs of consciousness and thus become artifacts of ego rather than intimations of eternity. Reifying Jung's rich metaphoric mosaic, which tracks the mysterious movement of energies, similarly reduces such metaphors as anima or shadow or complex to metaphysical concepts or the closed systems of allegories. Whatever the gods and goddesses are, or whatever the psyche intends through our dreams, is surely driven from those images when we encapsulate them in concepts. We then lose the tension of ambiguity that would allow images and dreams to suggest, intimate, and point beyond themselves toward the precincts of mystery.

Perhaps life is inherently meaningless, the raw flux of molecules forming, interacting, dissolving, and forming anew elsewhere. We have to be intellectually honest and admit this possibility and restrain the ego's nervous protest. Yet we find it difficult if not impossible to believe that such a purposeless concatenation of subatomic particles could have written the Ninth Symphony or the Declaration of Independence, or even built the airplanes that destroyed a small town, thus inspiring Picasso's *cri de coeur, Guernica*. But we do not have to answer this question here, or now, or ever; we can abide the tension of ambiguity in respectful service to mystery. Jung's concept of the archetype is an eminently useful tool for us to employ in service of meaning while still respecting the ambiguous character of the cosmos.

The concept of the archetype has attained such celebrity as to suffer the worst of two extremes—to be misinterpreted by otherwise intelligent persons, and to become a simplistic, popular term found at least monthly in such venues as *Time* magazine. The former have accused Jung of Lamarckism, a theory of organic evolution suggesting that what is learned in one generation is biologically transmitted to the next.[2] Rather, Jung speaks of the archetype as a formative process, more properly understood as a verb than a noun. The psyche has an apparent desire to render a raw flux of atoms intelligible and meaningful by sorting them into patterns. These patterns themselves form patterns, that is, archetypes create primal forms which are then filled with the contents unique to a particular culture, a particular artist, or a particular dreamer.

On the other hand, the popularization of the term *archetype* has so reduced its radical significance that at best the word means something important, universal, or moving. The idea of the archetype deserves better than this vague definition. Indeed, our capacity for symbol making differentiates us from all other natural species and makes our spirituality possible. It is our imaginal capacity (our ability to form images which carry energy) that constructs the requisite bridges to those infinite worlds which otherwise lie beyond our rational and emotional capacities. Without the archetypal imagination, we would have neither culture nor spirituality, and our condition would never have transcended brutish rutting in the dust en route to becoming dust itself.

We owe thanks to the Romantics for reminding us of the power of imagination, the power to create dynamic images (*Einbildungskraft*). In his *Biographia Literaria*, Samuel Taylor Coleridge differentiates "primary imagination," "secondary imagination," and "fancy." The last is what today we would call taste or, at best, aesthetics: the arrangement of form and color in pleasing proportions. But primary imagination, Coleridge suggests, was incarnated in Hebraic mythopoesis with Yahweh's primal "I Am that I Am." That is, such metaphor symbolizes the primordial constitutive act, the summoning up of something out of nothing, as in the Genesis announcement, "and God said it was good." For the Hebrew sensibility, then, the logos, or act of speech, symbolically represented the mystery of creation, especially the *creatio ex nihilo*, for to our limited human condition, nothing exists until we summon it to consciousness. Theretofore, creation may have existed independently, but it was beyond the sphere of human awareness and thus lay in the realm of non-being.

What Coleridge called the secondary imagination was what Jung means by the archetypal power, the capacity to echo, perhaps replicate, the original *creatio* through the generative power of an image. This generative power redeems image from the vagaries of human fancy, the velleities or inclinations of fashion, idiosyncrasy, and complex, and resonates with the power of divine creativity. As the poet Rilke claims, all of creation itself awaits this naming power to bring it into being.

Other so-called Romantics sought to redeem the worth of imagination from the *Aufklärung* where John Locke defined imagination as "decaying sense." According to Locke, the power to summon up the image of a tree depended upon the fading sensate inscriptions of past experience on the *tabula rasa* of the mind. However, for Goethe, Wordsworth, Keats, Shelley, and such thinkers as Kant and Schleiermacher, the imagination was the door to divinity. No one spoke more eloquently about the divine power of the imagination than the engraver William Blake. In a letter written in 1799 he noted, "to the eyes of the man of imagination Nature is imagination itself. As a man is so he sees . . . to me this world is all one continued vision."[3] For Blake and the Romantics, imagination is our highest faculty, not our reason, which is delimited by its own structures. Kant clearly proved that point in *A Critique of Pure Reason,* and Blake wittily remarked upon reason's limits in his lines "May God us keep / from single vision and Newton's sleep."[4] (While Blake admired the imaginative power of Newton and his dynamic metaphor for the cosmos, he despised the mechanistic mentality which it had begotten in Newton's successors, much as we today may decry the banishment of psyche from the practice of most psychology.) It is the archetypal imagination which, through the agencies of symbol and metaphor and in its constitutive power of imaging, not only creates the world and renders it meaningful but may also be a paradigm of the work of divinity. On another occasion Blake wrote with stunning emphasis: "The Eternal Body of Man is The Imagination / God himself that is The Divine Body . . . In Eternity All is Vision."[5]

Huston Smith, a historian of religion, once asked me this question: Does the archetype originate in the human psyche alone or does it have a function transcendent to individual experience?[6] While we cannot know the answer to that question definitively, I surmise that the archetypal function (remember archetype as verb) does both. It is the means by which the individual brings pattern and process to chaos, and it is the means by which the individual participates in those energies of the cosmos of which we are always a part. The archetypal imagination is, as Wordsworth defined it in "Tintern Abbey,"

> *a motion and a spirit, that impels*
> *all thinking things, all objects of all thought,*
> *and rolls through all things.*

Our intuition of this power fits what Wordsworth described as

> *a sense sublime*
> *of something far more deeply interfused,*
> *whose dwelling is the light of setting suns.*[7]

A practical manifestation of this process of archetypal imagining and a practical illustration of where our confusions arise can be seen in analysis.

I once worked with a Western physician who also practiced Eastern healing arts, both in private practice and at a major East Coast hospital. He knew Western surgery, pharmacology, nosology and diagnosis, emergency procedures, and family practice well. But out of his own curiosity and desire for a more balanced picture, he had undertaken formal study and certification in herbology, shiatsu, and acupuncture.

He felt that these two approaches to healing, while employing different root metaphors, were compatible and probably even more efficacious when combined. One system, employing mostly surgery and pharmacology, was allopathic, that is, invasive and counterposing certain effects with opposing, more powerful effects. The other was more homeopathic, operating from the view that health is the natural state and that the restoration of the ordinary flow of energy, called *ki, shi,* or *chi,* returned the person to that homeostasis we call health. While the physician believed that both Western and Eastern medicine were helpful, together they surely were even more powerful in activating the mystery of healing. In this scenario, the physician was not the cause of healing but rather the midwife of the organism's own intention.

But the physician faced continuing opposition from his frustrated medical colleagues. They not only demanded empirical data but also resisted the metaphors implicit in an alternative healing practice. While he was no stranger to, nor opponent of, standard research methods, he knew that what he had observed in his practice bespoke the efficacy of those Eastern healing traditions of several millennia. What he was confronting is common: the limited acceptance of the archetypal imagination and the anxiety with which the familiar picture is defended.

As director of the C. G. Jung Educational Center of Houston, I have had numerous opportunities to develop and find funding for programs that use the expressive arts to help ordinary individuals attain greater personal growth and development. These programs reach out to special populations, such as the homeless, the chronically or terminally ill, or disadvantaged children. Studies at Baylor College of Medicine have indicated that when children are traumatized, critical pathways of the brain are arrested, leading to intellectual and emotional impairment.

A growing body of evidence suggests that the expressive arts seem to reactivate those portions of the brain and reinstitute growth. Moreover, a study out of Stanford University indicated that the expressive arts are more efficacious than other interventions, be they after-school programs, sports, community projects, or medication. In working with an oncological facility, I learned that expressive arts restore some autonomy to an individual who feels disempowered by a catastrophic illness. Patients who engaged in artistic expression generally have greater tolerance of chemotherapy and other treatment modalities. Expressive arts may prolong life and palliate pain, but they also undoubtedly enhance spiritual well-being in the face of death. (Here again, the director of the program felt obliged to assemble hard data to justify these observed results to colleagues, so wedded were they to the common allopathic oncology treatments whose operative metaphors are grossly called "slash, burn, and poison.")

The point about the expressive and healing arts is not that they represent an exciting frontier for exploration, though they do. Rather, both Eastern healing models and the expressive arts are different ways of imagining. Why would sticking pins in someone ease a chronic condition elsewhere in the body? Why would painting or body movement restore portions of the brain's work? Why would imaging, sand tray, or other creative activities assist in the tolerance of institutionalized forms of treatment?

As suggested before, perhaps life is meaningless, but we are meaning-seeking creatures who are driven to understand it. Failing that, we attempt to form some meaningful relationship to life. We learn from archetypal psychology, from the core of primal religious experiences, from quantum physics, and from the artist's eye that all is energy. Matter is a dynamic, temporary arrangement of energy. Apparently, a religious symbol or a prayer, a work of art, or an expressive practice can so act on our psyche as to move that energy when it has been blocked, deadened, or split off.

The splitting of matter and spirit, which were last held together by the medieval alchemists, must now be knit together, and thoughtful theologians, imaginative physicists, and pragmatic physicians know that. The split between religion and science has been bigoted on both sides, ignorant, and has blocked the development of new healing modalities. The one-sidedness of organizing metaphors of East and West led one to preeminence in spirituality at the diminishment of the study of nature, and the other to prominence in the manipulation of the tangible world at the cost of soul. A dematerialized spirituality leads to the neglect of legitimate social issues, and the de-souling of nature leads to a bland, banal, and bankrupt superficiality.

But what is real, what is common to both sides of these dichotomies is not ideology but energy. All of them are energy systems. To be more specific, all of them are systematized images of energy. It does not matter whether the image is religious in character, purporting to embody the encounter with a transcendent reality, or material in character, purporting to describe the mystery of nature in incarnational flux. Each image presents itself to consciousness through what the philosopher Hans Vaihinger called a "useful fiction," an image whose purpose is to point beyond itself toward the mystery. As the mystery is by definition that which we cannot know, lest it no longer be the Mystery, our images are tools, not ends in themselves.

Underneath these cultural splits, the archetypal imagination seeks, through affectively charged images, to connect us to the flow of energy that is the heart and hum of the cosmos. With such images we have provisional access to the Mystery. Without them, we would remain locked forever within our bestial beginnings. Surely only fools and literalists would confuse the bridge toward the other shore with the shore itself, or the arrow with the target, or the desire with the object of desire.

Though we begin and end with the limits of our condition, an inexpressible hope, a yearning for connection, a desire for meaning, and a movement of energy toward healing drives us forward. Apparently, what is real and omnipresent is energy; what allows us to stand in relationship to that mystery is image; and what generates the bridge is an autonomous part of our own nature, the archetypal imagination. We are never more profoundly human than when we express our yearning, nor closer to the divine than when we imagine. This linkage with the infinite has of course been the intent of the great mythologies and religions, the healing creative and expressive arts, and the dreams we dream each night.

This inexplicable linkage was well known to the visionaries, the artists, and the prophets. We too are obliged to wrestle anew with the paradox that, while our condition remains fragile and sometimes terrible, we are nonetheless afforded a means by which to participate in the deepest mysteries of which we are a part and with which we long to connect.

Those who have tracked the history of Western thought from Plato through Newton through Hume and Kant have concluded that we can only know the answer to those questions which our mind is capable of asking. Our sciences are self-limiting imaginal systems, even when they are open-ended. The matters we know conform to matters which we can know, that is, which are within the confines of our capacities to know. Our sciences ask only the questions we are capable of knowing. When, however, we are visited by images which come from another place, from mysterious origin, we are opened to something larger than heretofore possible.

Consciousness is transformed by the encounter with mystery as invested in images theretofore foreign to it. In the world of contemporary deconstructionism, we believe that all knowledge is interpretation and all interpretation is subjective, prejudiced by unconscious determinants such class, gender, and Zeitgeist, and that no interpretation is final or authoritative. Thus, when the cosmos reveals itself to us, it is by way of the image foreign to consciousness. And it is through this encounter with the numinous that the power of the archetypal imagination makes growth possible.

Many years ago, long before I was a therapist, I played a role in the dream of a friend who was going through a terrible life crisis, not the least of which included the death of his child. In the dream I had placed a strip of masking tape on the end of his nose. He knew that I had not done this bizarre act as a joke or to make light of his Jobean dilemma. When we talked over the dream and focused on what Jung called the "obscure symbol," I spontaneously said, "Tom, what you are looking for is as near as the end of your nose." He had an immediate reaction—enlightenment—because his course was clear, albeit painful. He knew what he had to do.

Despite what we know to be the infinity of our yearning and the limits of our powers, we have been provided a means of communication with the mysteries. This power is as near as the end of one's nose. As Blake once expressed it:

> *I give you the end of a golden string,*
> *Only wind it into a ball:*
> *It will lead you in at Heaven's gate,*
> *Built in Jerusalem's wall.*[8]

CHAPTER 1

Religious Imaginings

Divine Morphologies

*If horses . . . had hands, or were able to draw with their
hands and do the work that man can do, horses would
draw the forms of gods like horses.*
—Xenophanes

*What we wish most to know, most desire, remains unknowable and lies
beyond our grasp.*

Houston poet Edward Hirsch's lines, "Stars are the white tears of
nothingness. / Nothingness grieves over the disintegrating gods" stir
in us a sense of wistfulness, pathos, longing and loss, even though they
are rationally inexplicable.[1] The personification of the stars, the evocation of "white tears," the grieving over lost certainties—all intimate
the inexplicable, which is the chief service of symbol and metaphor.
Compare the honesty of this feeling state, and the respect for the mystery which these lines portray, with the maudlin, infantilizing, and
hybristic utterances of the televangelists. Hirsch honestly reflects the
modern dilemma of living between myths, while the purveyors of one-
line theologies uphold the notion of the patriarchal parent. His lines
are part *cri de coeur*, part protest, and part expression of radical faith
in the immensity which lies both within and outside us. His is the honesty of Robert Frost, who observed,

> *They cannot scare me with their empty spaces*
> *Between stars—on stars where no human race is.*

> *I have it in me so much nearer home*
> *To scare myself with my own desert places.*[2]

Frost's evocation of images which summon affect and point beyond their conceptual husk toward the precincts of mystery testifies to the sincerity of the soul's intent. His condition is ours, and it reminds one of a comment made by the character Janie in a novel by Zora Neale Hurston. Janie said that there are two things all people have to do in their lives: "They got tuh go tuh God, and they got tuh find out about living for themselves."[3]

The core condition of our time has been manifest as a collective spiritual wound, one perhaps as traumatic as an amputation. (The theme of personal pathology or private wounding is discussed in chapter 4.) Jung noted that psychology was the last of the so-called social sciences to be invented because the insights which it seeks were previously in the domain of tribal mythologies and institutionalized religions. When moderns fell off the roof of the medieval cathedral, Jung wrote, they fell into the abyss of the Self. Affective linkage to the cosmos, nature, and the community was once available via tribal creation stories, heroic legends, and transformative rituals. With the loss of those connective rites and mythic images, the problem of identity and the task of cosmic location, or spiritual grounding, becomes an individual dilemma.

When the gods left Olympus, Jung suggested, they went into the unconscious and reign now in the solar plexus of the individual, or are projected into the world via the sundry sociopathies of a fragmented civilization.[5] Going back to Hirsch's lines, we see that they are elliptical, as much modernist art is, because the mythic ground has shifted from intimate relationship with nature, from stable social fabric, and from certainty of belief. Hirsch's metaphors, like T. S. Eliot's "this is the broken jaw of our lost kingdoms,"[6] communicate through their very "dis-location." In this existential chasm depth psychology necessarily finds its work, for spiritual dislocation is the chief wound which lies beneath the other wounds we treat with work, drugs, ideologies, or desperate love.

In his memoir, *Memories, Dreams, Reflections,* Jung offers a perspective which is very helpful to us:

The need for mythic statements is satisfied when we frame a view of the world which adequately explains the meaning of human existence in the cosmos, a view which springs from our psychic wholeness, from the cooperation between the conscious and the unconscious. Meaninglessness inhibits fullness of life and is therefore equivalent to illness. Meaning makes a great many things endurable—perhaps everything. No science will ever replace myth, and a myth cannot be made out of any science. For it is not that "God" is a myth, but that myth is the revelation of a divine life in man.[7]

This paragraph is very rich and will reward us upon further consideration.

First, Jung suggests, our deepest need is for a sense of spiritual, or psychic locus, by which he means a sense of belonging to a superordinate reality, a perspective on one's place in the larger scheme of things, a confirmation of one's role, task, and purpose in striding this planet. When Jung visited the pueblo in Taos, he learned from Ochwiay Biano, Chief Mountain Lakes, that his people, like the Elongyi tribe of Kenya, rose in the morning and spit in their palms, thereby presenting their soul-stuff to the sun to welcome it in an expression of sympathetic magic. Jung marveled that the people of the pueblo knew why they were here. What seems naive to the traveler offers most what that restless traveler is seeking—a reason for being here.

Going beyond the fact of our desire to connect with the cosmos, Jung argues that the desire itself rises from our psychic wholeness. We are all the carriers of that energy which fires the cosmos, what Dante called "The love that moves the sun and the other stars."[8] Or, as the ancient smaragdine tablet(which explained the secret of the cosmos) of Hermes Trismegistus (also known as Thoth, the Egyptian god who invented writing) had it, "Things above are copies of things below. Things below are copies of things above." Thus, as carriers of the same energy which animates the cosmos, we employ the archetypal imagination as the power of constitutive ordering which makes meaning possible. This "transcendent function," as Jung called it, not only links us with ourselves, bridging the conscious world with the unconscious through the venues of somatic symptom, affect, vision, and dream image, but also links us to superordinate reality through the symbolic powers.[9]

The loss of symbolic connection to self or cosmos, Jung suggests in the excerpted paragraph, is the chief source of our illness. As he so often asserted, neurosis is suffering without meaning and the flight from authentic being. The loss of tribal symbols, and the linkage with the transcendent which they provided, obliged the meaning task to invert as personal neurosis.

The recovery of meaning not only relocates a person in a larger order of things but also supports a sense of personal identity and directs energies in life-serving ways. (I can personally attest to encounters with these transcendent energies through working on my own psyche, with the psychic life of others, and in the mysterious, mythopoeic energies which fashion our dreams. These encounters with transcendent energies are fundamentally inexplicable, but they are undeniable and require an honest person to witness with humility and awe.)

Jung further observed that science, for all its worthy powers of learning and methodology, cannot create meaning. Meaning is the epiphenomenal component of depth experience. When we recall that the Greek word *psyche* means *soul*, then we are obliged to discern that the tragedy of most modern psychologies, which divide the person into behaviors, cognitions, and psychobiologies—each true, but each partial—is that their practitioners ignore the most immediate reality of all, namely, the suffering of the soul, as manifest in the consulting room.

The bankruptcy of modern psychology is its flight from the soul, and therefore from the transcendent task of meaning. Such a denial of depth is a failure of nerve in the face of largeness. Similarly, most theologies have substituted the powers of institutions and clerical dogma for the immediacy and idiosyncrasy of personal experience. We cannot transfer experience to each other; each of us has got to go to "God" and find out about living for ourselves, as Hurston reminded us. Just as Jung reminded us that "psychotherapy can be a mere makeshift for the avoidance with the reality of the psyche," so we regretfully conclude that the chief motive of many religious institutions is the avoidance of actual spiritual experience.

Both psychology and institutional religion have fallen into the shadow problem where fear of the living, dynamic, sometimes anarchic psyche prevails. Worse, psychology and religion have addressed their fear of the psyche by attempting to apply power and ego control, to promote ideology rather than mythology. As understandable as these fear-based stratagems may be, they will of course be overthrown by those powers we call the gods and by the autonomy of the unconscious. As Jung asserts, "The archetype behind a religious idea has, like every instinct, its specific energy, which it does not lose even if the conscious mind ignores it."[11] This is why the person who views the world in depth, who reads its ciphers, as Karl Jaspers urged, sees the movement of soul everywhere, however unconsciously processed.

Myth is not created; it is the phenomenological dramatization of our encounter with depth. As Jung concludes, "myth is the revelation of a divine life in man."[12] This divine life is expressed through the psyche's archetypal process, which lifts images up and out of the flux of nature to serve as mediatory bridges to the cosmos. In speaking of the archetype Jung means something elemental. Just as there are instincts for biological survival and social interaction, there are instincts for spiritual connection as well. Just as our physical and social needs seek satisfaction, so the spiritual instincts of this human animal are expressed through the power of images to evoke affective response. Anyone who has worked with dreams and encountered the powers transcendent to ego must have some inclination of the power such images once held for our tribal ancestors. As Jung concludes, "Myths and fairytales give expression to unconscious processes, and their retelling causes these processes to come alive and be recollected, thereby reestablishing the connection between conscious and unconscious. What the separation of the two psychic halves means, the psychiatrist knows only too well. He knows it as dissociation of the personality, the root of all neuroses."[13]

This dissociation of the individual personality we know by the ugly and misleading term *neurosis,* just as T. S. Eliot observed its collective cultural form in what he called "the dissociation of sensibility"—the chief spiritual dilemma of society.[14]

The archetypal imaging power represents an aspect of our participation in the divine. Jung writes: "The archetypes are the numinous structural elements of the psyche and possess a certain autonomy and specific energy which enables them to attract, out of the conscious mind, those contents which are best suited to themselves. The symbols act as transformers, their function being to convert libido from a 'lower' to a 'higher' form."[15]

These two rich sentences bear further attention. Note those key words *numinous* and *structural*. The idea of the numinous is buried in its etymology. The word of origin means to nod, to summon, to intimate; that is, the numinous is autonomous and is seeking us, soliciting the attention of our consciousness. Secondly, the psyche brings structure to this frenetic dance of atoms so that we might stand in ordered relationship to that flux. This order makes meaning possible; it is the requisite for consciousness.

Moreover, as the student of dreams knows well, the invisible energy of the psyche scavenges the known and the unknown worlds for images to become hosts for meaning. Such image-husks are filled with energy and present themselves dynamically for the possibility of conscious discernment. In addition to creating consciousness alone, these images activate, summon, and direct libido and energy in service to the developmental and transcendent needs of the organism. This effect is experienced in rites of passage, in living religious symbols, and in affectively charged life experiences which move and confound us. Through the autonomous formation of symbols and archetypal imagination, we move to ancient rhythms and play out ancient dramas, whether we know it or not.

The deceptions of modern culture tempt the conscious mind to serve immediate gratification, but Jung has noted that, in the end, such ideologies as materialism, hedonism, and narcissism simply do not work, and they do not connect. Meaning only comes "when people feel that they are living the symbolic life, that they are actors in the divine drama. That gives the only meaning to human life; everything else is banal and you can dismiss it. A career, the producing of children, all are *maya* [illusion] compared with that one thing, that your life is meaningful."[16]

We live in a spiritually impoverished time, and Jung argues "that it would be far better stoutly to avow our spiritual poverty, our symbollessness, instead of feigning a legacy to which we are not the legitimate heirs at all."[17] Although we have lost our spiritual connection, we have not lost our spiritual desire. In the same way, although we are without gods, they have not disappeared. The problem is simply that the images generally available to us have lost the power to point beyond themselves and thus to connect us with the mystery, although we may cling to those image-husks with fundamentalist fervor to mask our disquietude. Even Jesus noted this tendency when he said to his disciples, "My Kingdom is spread all over the earth, and you do not see it."[18]

While a person who works in sincere dialogue with others, submits to the urges of creative impulse within, and tracks the invisible world through his or her dreams will have a living spirituality, this person is, sadly, atypical in our time. For all of us, the symbolic world is as near as tonight's dream, or even in a deepened understanding of our neurotic symptoms. We have, however, the opportunity to take a historical trip to recollect how meaning is found, how the gods and goddesses rise invisibly from the depths, and how we are part of a timeless drama.

The inescapable solipsism of our condition often imprisons us in the limits of our narrow frame of conscious life and biographical exposure. When we approach the religion of others we find ourselves unmoved or inclined to condescend to anything that seems foreign to our experience. When we examine and compare the religious, spiritual, or psychological expressions of others to our own, however, we find that the same process of archetypal imagination is at work. It becomes obvious that despite the disparity of time, geography, and Zeitgeist, we are all part of one psychic family.

Consider, for example, how we conjure with the idea of God. By definition we are constrained as finite beings before the infinite and are constitutionally incapable of revealing much more than our own psychology and prejudices in our theological utterances. Thus, the Wholly Other, to use Karl Barth's phrase from *Das Kirklichle Dogmatik,* remains wholly other. Nonetheless, how humans have searched for and formulated their sense of transcendent reality provides clues, not only to the mystery of Mystery but also to the capacity of the archetypal imagination to provide figural access to the Divine. Let four quite disparate examples serve to illustrate this imaginative power at work in bringing us into proximity with the Wholly Other.

Western philosophy could be said to begin with the exclamation of the pre-Socratic Thales: *panta theon plere,* or "everything is full of gods!" In this formulation Thales witnesses the depth and dynamism of all things; he exercises the spiritual eye, the archetypal, figural imagination. He says, in effect, "Look, look, see there; it is alive!" In the post-Newtonian universe, Blake lamented that without wonder, atoms bumping up against other atoms leads only to entropy, even death. The quantum physicist, working on the edge of emerging models of matter, sees energy disappear into something altogether different. The physicist can then recover a sense of primal awe in the recognition that, indeed, everything is full of gods. This use of metaphor is simply the best way to be scientific, that is, to pursue *scientia* or a deeper knowledge of things as they are and as they may be. "See there; it lives" is the credo of the scientist, and his or her use of metaphor is the resource used to build a bridge from conscious life to the unknown depths. As Carl Kerenyi notes, "The fundamental word of this theology is *theos.* From a strictly methodological point of view it is consoling that in order to understand *theos,* no known or unknown god-concept, no 'idea of god,' need be introduced. All we have to do is start from an experience in which this word is spoken predicatively."[19] In other words, the word *god* is not a concept, nor a presumed metaphysical construct; it is an encounter, an experience with the vitalistic cosmos.

In the same phenomenological state as Thales, the Jesuit poet Gerard Manley Hopkins celebrated the variety and flux of life. He concludes the poem "Pied Beauty" with praise for the humming energy which lies beneath the world of appearances:

> *All things counter, original, spare, strange;*
> *Whatever is fickle, freckled (who knows how?)*
> *With swift, slow; sweet, sour; adazzle, dim;*
> *He fathers-forth whose beauty is past change:*
> *Praise Him.*[20]

"Who knows how" indeed. The apprehension of the divine is found in the spiritual reading of the mundane. To the spiritual eye, the *quidditas* of things becomes an aperture into infinite mystery whereby energy animates matter.

When one considers the name and nature of Zeus, one finds many tracks which lead from Asia and Europe to the Indo-Germanic language which is the mother stream of our speech. All of those tracks together constitute the etymology of *light*, both word and concept. How are we who are finite to conjure with the infinite without resorting to the instrument of metaphor? We might employ any concrete image to summon up this unfathomable mystery of light, but most would fall short of the numinosity to which it points. The ubiquity and necessity of the sun could not have failed to impress our forebears as the source of life, the source of growth, the light which holds back the terrifying dark, and so on. Such associations point toward the mystery of the energy with which the world is charged.

Kerenyi further discovered that the original metaphor, which is always a radical, phenomenological encounter, meant not so much light as "the moment of lighting up."[21] Thus, light as a concept is only a noun, a husk; the lightening is an experience. Day versus night, light versus dark, and energy versus entropy is profound, but the dynamic encounter with the lightening is even more powerful. Thus, the experience involves being struck, seeing the bolt, or feeling its jolt.

This movement from concept to numinous experience is the difference between the Job who was a good, pious boy, obedient to a code of ethics, and the Job who discovered the living God in terror and wonder. He moves from concept to experience. Many prattle on about psychotherapy, whether to praise it or denigrate it. Unless one has encountered the autonomous, disruptive power of the psyche, one is merely full of talk, full of what Whitehead called the dance of bloodless categories. Jung was very clear about such a difference. As he wrote in 1959 in an astounding letter about his use of the word *god*, "It is an apt name given to all overpowering emotions in my own psychic system, subduing my own conscious will and usurping control over myself. It is the name by which I designate all things which cross my willful path violently and recklessly, all things which upset my subjective views, plans, and intentions and change the course of my life for better or worse."[22]

This is not a definition of the divine found in many breviaries or catechisms, but it is a profoundly respectful account of the author's experience with the numinous, the autonomous Other which lies outside the frame of conscious control and occasions ever new possibilities of depth encounter. When Jung defines neurosis as a "neglected god," he means no denigration of anyone's theology nor scandal to behaviorists; rather, he wishes to accord the depth energies within us a larger measure of respect than generally afforded by the ego. He knows, as does every depth psychologist, that such energies neglected, repressed, split off, or projected, will simply find their own autonomous and often disruptive venues for expression. As nature will not be mocked, so the dynamic energies which course through us will neither be suppressed nor controlled forever, lest they in time break forth as monsters.

Thus, Kerenyi is insisting that Zeus is the image which arises out of the experience of the sun and is not the sun itself. Zeus later became a sun god through the extension of these natural associations, but he was originally the experience of being suffused with light itself; he was not the light but the experience of light.

Coming down a quite different path, the poet Wallace Stevens wrote in his poem "Sunday Morning" of the contemporary spiritual dilemma from a postmodern perspective. Rather than seek the divine in institutional or dogmatic form, he images himself as a savage, dancing in adoration of the pagan sun: "Not as a god, but as a god might be, / naked among them, like a savage source."[23]

This urgency to personify the cosmos is the primal religious need to connect with the Mystery. The etymology of the word *religion* reveals two sources, one meaning "to bind back to something" (*re-ligare*) and the other "to take into careful account" (*religere*). The former impulse is toward reuniting with the source from which one has become estranged, and the latter is to respect the *gravitas* of that mystery. When Stevens writes "not as a god, but as a god might be," he is both acknowledging the postmodern recognition of the husk which has lost its sacred energy and also affording an existential respect for the power of the numinous. To dance about the sun as a savage sensibility, Stevens suggests, will perhaps bring one closer to re-evoking that numinous mystery than would pious acts sanctified by dogma.

Jung, as usual, has anticipated this discussion and even uses the image of the sun to explain:

> Primitive man is not much interested in objective explanations of the obvious, but he has an imperative need—or rather, his unconscious psyche has an irresistible urge—to assimilate all outer sense experiences to inner, psychic events. It is not enough for the primitive to see the sun rise and set; this external observation must at the same time be a psychic happening: the sun in its course must represent the fate of a god or hero who, in the last analysis, dwells nowhere except in the soul of man.[24]

This need to assimilate, to internalize, is the need we all have to render the world personal and experiential in a spiritual and meaningful way. Among the fifteen or so subject areas in which analysts are examined at the Jung Institute in Zurich is the psychology of primitive cultures. As the word *primitive* is out of fashion now, one might substitute the word *primordial*. We were asked to demonstrate knowledge of many topics of anthropological significance because the human psyche has not changed. There are certain forms and motifs common to all cultures irrespective of cultural overlay, and the nature of primordial thinking about profound experience remains common to us all. We see magical thinking, projection, conversion, transference, projective identification, spirit possession, and a host other psychic phenomena manifest not only in psychotic process but in everyday life as well.

Yet the failure to internalize primary experience is why the light has gone out in so many religious and academic institutions. It is not enough to have the received image; it must retain the power to move one personally, direct libido in service of personal development or cultural sublimation, and stir the heart while persuading the brain. Moreover, such images must further contribute to one's sense of participation in that divine drama of which Jung spoke. Hence the ascent, the pleroma, and the descent of that brilliant gaseous mass in the sky is analogized so that we might understand both the vital principle we call gods and goddesses as well as something about the life-transit of each of us.

In the death and rebirth of the sun, in the defeat of darkness, in the oxymoronic "eternality of evanescence" are found the essential and universal experiences of otherwise individualized lives. Jung continues, "they are symbolic expressions of the inner, unconscious drama of the psyche which becomes accessible to man's consciousness by way of projection—that is, mirrored in the events of nature. The projection is so fundamental that it has taken several thousand years of civilization to detach it in some measure from its outer object."[25]

To read the cosmos, then, we need to read the psychic life of individuals. Or, put another way, we read myth to learn what is in the human soul; we read the human soul to learn the dynamic laws and principles of the mythic cosmos. Jung asks why psychology is the youngest of the empirical sciences and why we did not long before discover the unconscious and raise up its treasure-house of eternal images. His answer? "Simply because we [previously] had a religious formula for everything psychic."[26] Because of this progressive separation of psychic life from nature and the result, a de-souled cosmos, we have been obliged to invent psychology to inquire after the velleities of the soul turned in upon itself. No wonder Eliot observed in *The Waste Land* that we live amid "a heap of broken images."

How far removed this is from that time when the Greek world could still experience the lighting up as both an inner and an outer experience—an experience which could once be evoked in the utterance of the sacred word *Zeus*. Such an experience is truly religious, in both senses of the word, for there is a re-connective process and a deeply considered event.

Added to this moment when inner and outer theophany are one is the experience of the *daimon,* a most personal encounter with the divine. The daimon may be seen as both transpersonal and intrapersonal. The daimon is the intermediary agency, as in the Christian mythologem of the Holy Spirit, yet it was experienced in intensely personal ways so that each of us might claim to have our particular daimon.

Surely each of us has had from childhood on a deeply intuited sense of an interior Other who was manifest in sundry ways, who could not be summoned at will but was one's familiar, and who knew us, and knew other matters, more deeply than we could comprehend. Most of us have lost contact with that presence, and surely one of the greatest tasks of therapy is to reintroduce a person to his or her daimon—the individual yet transpersonal dimension which drives us, wants something of us, and constitutes our linkage to largeness. I recall one woman who called her daimon by the anagram TWIHAT, standing for "that which I have always thought." When it spoke, through dreams, sudden insights, and openings to the world beneath this world, she listened.

Hidden in the etymological recesses of the gods and goddesses are radical (that is, fundamental) insights into the nature of reality. In fact, we could define these divine beings archetypally, symbolically speaking, as the affect-laden, highly charged, numinous images which arise out of a depth experience. For this reason, they are present in love and war, as we all know, and even in those experiences that arise out of the psychopathology of everyday life and which Jung dared call "god." We smile and nod in recognition at the name Poseidon, whose eponymous metaphor means earth-shaker. Whoever set out on Homer's wine-dark sea, or stood close by while black sails sank beneath the horizon, or trembled amid the great power which shook beneath one's feet knows the metaphor of earth-shaker well. Or one thinks of Ceres, the goddess of grains, from whom we get our diurnal cereal. She sacrifices her body, which is broken on the threshing floor, alchemically transformed into bread, and then inexplicably converted into sinew, brain matter, and the yearnings of the soul. Who could account for these things? Who cannot but stand and praise with the heart (and hopefully a ready metaphor) what will forever confound the mind?

The development of modernism represents the diminishment of the numinosity of these root metaphors and their incremental replacement with artifacts of intellect. As tools of the intellect, these root metaphors are easily manipulated, but they are less and less able to stir the heart or move the soul. Kerenyi delineates this declension:

Human experience does not always give rise immediately to ideas. It can be reflected in images or words without the mediation of ideas. Man reacted inwardly to his experience before he became a thinker. Prephilosophical insights and reactions to experience are taken over and further developed by thought, and this process is reflected in language. . . . Language itself can be wise and draw distinctions through which experience is raised to consciousness and made into a prephilosophic wisdom common to all those who speak that language.[27]

To summarize, a primal experience begets an image which is the carrier of the mystery. For a time, a moment or a millennium, that image remains suffused with energy and may be evoked to summon the primary experience or a simulacrum of it. As time is the enemy of symbol, and the deities have their own agenda, the energy leaves the image, which remains an artifact of mind, a husk which once the gods and goddesses inhabited. The oldest of religious blasphemies is the literalization of the husk and its worship, when the energy has already gone elsewhere. This is idolatry, and its servant is that reification which protects itself against the gods and goddesses by worshiping their graves. When such vital linkage leaves the individual, he or she suffers neurosis; when it leaves the tribe, it occasions a cultural crisis, with all of those sociopathies which beset us today. The suffering occasioned by the loss of the light is what made analytic psychology necessary. It is a means of helping the individual find his or her own way back to the precincts of numinosity.

The Insect God of Dung

On my desk in Houston there is a four-inch-long alabaster carving of a scarab. Those of us who were raised in the Western religious tradition, which is to say, the dogmas, rituals, conventional art, and defining institutions of the medieval and Renaissance eras, may find it hard to conjure with the idea of a dung beetle as an image of divinity. Not only is it lacking in grandeur, but it hardly seems to exalt or glorify the idea of the eternal. Yet in this lowliest of creatures, we once again find the archetypal imagination at work. Even Blake, in "The Songs of Innocence and Experience," had to wonder if God had intended some sort of private joke when he made "our places of joy excrementitious." Taking a clue from the Egyptian imagination, however, we find that the most religious of ideas—the idea of death and resurrection—emerges out of the humblest of matter.

The lowly but sacred beetle (*Scarabaeus sacer*) serves as the object of imaginal exfoliation when it is found in sarcophagi and when it seemingly arises out of dung. What idea could be more profound than this, that out of death new life emerges? The sun, which is born over and over again, similarly suggested death and rebirth and the natural rhythm of things, and the great solar disk is central to Egyptian iconography. And these two symbols, scarab and sun, are logically linked; the Egyptians observed that the dung beetle laid its larvae in dung, rolled that dung into a ball, and pushed it into holes which it had dug for this purpose. After a period of gestation, the beetle pulls the hardened ball, reminiscent of the sun-disk, back out into the sun. When the sun's rays dry and crack open this *vas hermeticum*, new life emerges.

How powerfully these two images, of the dying and reborn sun and the beetle who brings life out of dead matter, speak to the primal imagination. The deity Kheperi, the god of transformations, was frequently depicted with a scarab beetle on his head or a scarab for his head. In modern Sudan, the scarab beetle is still dried and mixed into fertility potions for women.[28]

Some individuals might think such imagery arose from those with too much time on their hands, and they would be right. But today we have too little time on our hands. So distracted are we by the pace of modern life that we grow separated from the natural world and our wonder before it. As the pace of life accelerated in early modern Europe four hundred years ago, the mathematician/theologian Blaise Pascal wrote in his *Pensées* that the secret task of civilization was to offer *divertissement* or "distraction," lest we grow terrified of being wholly present to ourselves.

Before moving to Texas I had an office with a cathedral ceiling and glass walls on three sides. As I sat for a decade in the same chair, at the same hours, day in and day out, I became aware of the transits of the sun. While such solar progression would have been imperceptible to the distracted person, I began to note how different objects received a unique angle of light and took on various textures every day, as the hours and seasons passed. In a year, of course, we returned to the beginning and started anew. This simplest of observations, which any shepherd on any hillside would have similarly experienced, filled me with awe and stirred a sense of participation in the Mystery.

Our time in the changing lights of this cycling sun is so brief, but this cycle is eternal. When we become present to such feeling-laden experience, we have religious experience, that is, we are reconnected, and we observe with *gravitas*. However conventional, or even obvious, my observation, it was a moving reminder to me of both personal evanescence and at the same time participation in the archetypal rounds. So it must have been to the Egyptian who observed the lowly beetle in its instinctual rounds and became aware that we truly are, as Jung said, participants in a sacred drama. Surely this is why we long to visit the ocean or stand before a mountain range—to return to our small place before the large, to recover a sense of cosmic proportion.

It was from the French structural anthropologists Lucien Levy-Bruhl and Claude Levi-Strauss that we gained a new appreciation for the "primitive mind" (better termed "primal mind," which does not imply inferiority). In contrast to the primal mind, we as moderns have fallen into ethnocentrism by valuing a particular form of conceptualizing, most commonly a cause-effect thought process: A begets B. The meaning of A and B arises out of the predication of B by A and, increasingly in America, the cost to produce B from A.

For the primal mind, however, the meaning of a concept is not derived from causality but from imaginative association. Thus, a modern mind would hear a door slam and conclude that the sound meant the door was now shut. But the primal imagination may associate the sound with the event of passage through that door.

In this example of the door, the primal imagination saw life emerging from the basest of matter and was stirred to grasp a dynamic truth. Although the modern mind would label this idea illogical, it in fact follows a logos of perhaps a higher order, the logic of imaginative association. The image is not itself the concept, as the modern mind would have it, but rather what the image may stir in the unconscious, or what aperture it may open to depth.

While the modern mind can produce great wonders, and great horrors, it can just as easily sever itself from the archetypal roots of our spiritual nature, which sustained and nourished us through the centuries. The power to connect with the transpersonal will surely prove even greater than the power to fractionate. The chief cause of our psychological distress, our spiritual malaise, is the deracination of our archetypal rooting in nature and the poverty of affective, imaginative association with the passing wonders of the world.

The Latchkey to Eternal Life

Once while touring Ireland my wife and I visited a burial site named New Grange, which had been unearthed perhaps a hundred miles northwest of Dublin. What was once thought simply to be a hill was found to be a domelike structure measuring about three hundred feet across the top. To enter the tomb, one walks down a narrow tunnel perhaps fifty feet into the earth. Therein lies a chamber which served as a burial place for an unknown civilization that pre-dated the Celts and the Egyptian pyramids. The guide turned off the one electric light in the chamber and allowed us to be in total darkness in the three thousand-year-old tomb, after telling us that the entire structure was composed of cantilevered boulders with no mortise-and-tenon, nail, or super-glue holding it together. A single sneeze might do it, I thought; after all, why would we expect any building to last three millennia?

As we stood in this place I had three thoughts in this order. First, and most obviously, I was in awe of the engineering which had created this marvel, a cantilevered dome of stone upon stone that outlasted its engineers and testified to the window on eternity. Next, there was a latchkey hole in the eastern quadrant of the ceiling. Between December 21 and 25 light streams through that hole and illuminates the entire chamber for approximately fifteen minutes. So, secondly, I marveled at the astronomical sophistication of the builders of that place, to have discerned so accurately the movement of the heavens that long ago. But thirdly, I shuddered, not from being in a place of death, but rather from being in a place of resurrection. I knew that I was in the presence of the archetypal imagination, the realm of the Great Mother cycle of mythology.

Such archetypal imagery bespeaks the greatest of religious ideas: birth, ascendance, death, and then rebirth. In the place of the dead, at the time of the winter solstice, at the time of the star of Bethlehem, at the time of the candles of Chanukah, at the time when there is little light, when we are in the dark realm, we are nonetheless reminded that the planet is already spiraling back toward light, toward spring, toward resurrection. To this moment I remain moved by the power of that imaginative linkage. To see in the dark time the rebirth of this scintilla of light, to bring one's dead to the place where such a profound mythologem could be ritualized and celebrated, is to be an actor in the sacred drama. How could we not honor those who felt such a deep connection to the fundamental rhythm of nature, to the death and rebirth of divine nature, and to the wonder of our own being which partakes of the same energy?

The theologian Paul Tillich once observed that the chief curse of our time is not that we are evil, though often we are, but that we are banal, superficial. The recovery of depth will never come through an act of intellect, unless that intellect is in service to wonder. We can recover depth, however, by opening ourselves to the numinous which nods at us and invites us. We can also use our imaginative power to seize such moments of beckoning and the images which rise spontaneously from them.

Magic and Mistletoe

In the nineteenth century there was a substantial interest in the exploration of antique civilizations, Heinrich Schliemann's explorations of what he believed to be Agamemnon's palace at Troy being the most notable. The brothers Grimm traversed the Germanic states and transcribed tales of the spinning wheel, the *Märchen,* which we today call the fairy tales. Concurrent with the erosion of literal Christian beliefs under the combined onslaught of new methods of biblical scholarship and the epochal discoveries of Darwin, an interest in folk wisdom intensified as individuals sought to recover spiritual insights from other traditions. From the founding of The Theosophical Society in London in 1875 and the emergence of analytical psychology at the end of that century, alternative paths to spiritual insight opened.

Interest in the great mythological traditions culminated in 1890 with the publication of Sir James George Frazer's magisterial *The Golden Bough: A Study in Magic and Religion*. While all mythological, alchemical, and folk culture motifs are vast treasuries for those who would learn the dynamics of psychological process, we will focus now on the idea of the golden bough. What was it? Why was it important? We know that the golden bough was carried by Aeneas in his *catabasis* to the lower world. But what was the play of imagination which produced this image, and what truths perseverate through time?

Frazer was a scholar of his age. While his learning was immense, his cultural bias seems dated today. Curious as he was at the plethora of images available from antiquity, he tended to consider the contemporary religions superior, and humanity more evolved. (This more evolved culture would shortly slaughter itself at little villages like Verdun, Ypres, and Passchendaele, and in the Argonne Forest, but Frazer could not imagine such, though Dostoevski did. Nor could he imagine that the land of *Dichter und Denker*—poets and thinkers—would become the nation of *Mörder und Henker*—murderers and hangmen). Frazer is led to anticipate the idea of the archetypal imagination through the replication of mythologems from culture to culture. He concluded, "recent researches into the early history of man have revealed the essential similarity with which, under many superficial differences, the human mind has elaborated its first crude philosophy of life . . . producing in varied circumstances a variety of institutions specifically different but generically alike."[29]

Frazer's interest in magic arose out of his encounter with a certain kind of thinking, which I would call the imaginative power. He tended to consider such thinking primitive when compared with cognitive, syllogistic thought. But his delineation of sympathetic magic and contagious magic is still helpful to us.

The idea of sympathetic magic is based on the notion of similarity. For example, couples might copulate in newly planted fields to rouse the powers of nature or to evoke the gods to similarly fructify. Or they might sacrifice a plant, an animal, or an old king in order to simulate and stimulate the cycle of sacrifice wherein new life arises out of death. Contagious magic is based on the idea of contact. Things joined, or which are contiguous, are forever influential on each other. We know the truth of this when we observe the staying power of parental complexes or the fact that divorce does not end a marriage. What has been powerfully joined, for good or ill, continues to influence one with the other in perpetuity.

What Frazer calls magic is the effort to conjure with the invisible world, whether intentional or not. While magical thinking—the assumption that my thoughts or actions can have an effect on the other— may strike us as naive and misguided, we have to recall the power of complexes, projections, scapegoating, psychic possession, and transference phenomena, which Jung helped identify, to admit that, indeed, there is such movement of invisible energy for which the word magic was once used.

Jungians puzzle other schools of psychology with their interest in such antique material, but part of Jung's genius was to see the human psyche as a hologram. Wheresoever it is at work, it leaves the imprint of its pervasive dynamics. To learn of those fundamental psychic processes which we all embody, suffer, and are driven by, we may steep ourselves in the *Märchen*. To study such material is to uncover the recurrent paradigms of psychic process for individual therapy. Frazer's magic is primary psychic process, and what he considers amusing but interesting mythic motifs, we see constituting the residue of that archetypal imagination which renders the world meaningful.

Jung would not publish his theory of archetypes until 1912 in *Symbols of Transformation*. Those who deny the archetypal imagination simply have not immersed themselves in the thesaurus of images available, from East and West and from the ancient world, nor have they sharpened the eye to see those same motifs in modern dress.

The magical thought that "like heals like," what we call homeopathic medicine, certainly occurred to our ancestors. The golden bough is one example. Associated with the sacred groves of Artemis/Diana, the hunter goddess of the woods, it derives from the mistletoe which was cut at the winter solstice. In time it turns yellow, that is, golden. Mistletoe's presumed powers supposedly arose from the fact that it seemed neither tree nor bush. It dwelt in the in-between, between heaven and earth, and therefore partook of two worlds, possessing the power to heal or destroy. (Buried in the idea of *pharmakon,* from which we derive "pharmacology," is similarly the notion of killing or curing by ingesting certain substances.) The green world mistletoe seemed feminine to the antique imagination even as the tree around which it was circled seemed masculine. Again, one sees the interaction of two worlds. That it was green at the time of the winter solstice further stirred the association with the death/rebirth theme already discussed. The yellowing of the green was seen as a solar residue and thus, even more in the mixing of solar and lunar, the carrier of the numinous. What better imago of healing and of illumination of darkness, then, than magic and mistletoe? What better guide, as Aeneas illustrated, through the dark descents into night?

What images do we have of healing that intimate for us contact with the mysteries? Today we swallow the magical pill manufactured in New Jersey and fervently hope that like will continue to cure like. It is still magic, and as we know from the placebo effect, it works all the better the more our heart and imagination embrace the treatment. As modern medicine is coming to acknowledge, we would be better to embrace the placebo effect as a clue to the power of psyche's healing intent than dismiss it as a bizarre and idiosyncratic phenomenon. We know from shamanism to the present that a key element in healing is belief in the power of an agency to effect healing, whether that agency be a Tlingit shaman, a Navajo sand painting, a person in a white coat at a high-tech medical center, or a pill created in a huge factory.

In examining these four motifs, the name and nature of Zeus, the insect god of dung, the latchkey to eternity, and the link between magic and mistletoe, we are visiting a place in the human psyche where nothing has changed. We think our age is advanced, and technologically it is, but at the cost of that fragile linkage to the animistic powers of nature. Our capacity to open our own imagination to take in the images of other times and places, other human beings like us, reconnects us with ourselves in the end, for we are they, and they are us. We remember that the symbolic life, as Jung called it, occurs wheresoever we engage in depth. We learn so much more about the actual functioning of the human psyche—its employment of projection, magical thinking, and the like—than modern textbooks of behavior, cognition, and pharmacology even attempt. We find that we are no more advanced where it matters than were our ancestors who may have huddled in fear and cold caves, in forests or tundras, but they had a connection to the transcendent powers which we ignore at our peril.

The archetypal imagination is the means by which we encounter the divine and how it may be reborn in us. As Jung writes,

> The mediatorial product [i.e., image or symbol] ... forms the raw material for a process not of dissolution but of construction, in which thesis and antithesis both play their part. In this way it becomes a new content that governs the whole attitude, putting an end to the division and forcing the energy of the opposites into a common channel. The standstill is overcome and life can flow on with renewed power towards new goals.[30]

Out of the tension of opposites, the new thing, the third, is where the gods and humans meet, where developmental healing occurs, and where meaning will still be found. What our predecessors lived, we have now rendered conscious. While consciousness can be a hindrance to transformation, it may also enable us to recover a respect for the imaginal world and to confess a humbling need to track those images to see what they may be asking of us.

CHAPTER 2

Literary Imaginings

Envisioned Logos

Poetry heals the wounds reason creates.
—Novalis

What we wish most to know, most desire, remains unknowable and lies beyond our grasp. In this chapter we will celebrate the power of speech to assist us in our task of articulating this deep longing.

To my mind, while I love the work of many poets from many lands, none surpasses that of Prague-born Rainer Maria Rilke for depth of insight, aesthetic achievement, and visionary ambition. If I had only two boxes of books to take to the proverbial desert island, one of them would be the *Collected Works* of Jung and the other would be the prose and poetry of Rilke, born the same year as Jung, in 1875. Both would offer inexhaustible explorations of the mystery of the psyche, no matter how long one remained on that island.

In the previous chapter I did not intend to denigrate the power of language or to privilege phenomenological experience over consciousness. Indeed, we recall the observation of Kerenyi that "Language itself can be wise and draw distinctions through which experience is raised to consciousness and made into a prephilosophic wisdom common to all those who speak that language."[1] We are using language even now to activate enhanced awareness of, and the possibility of, enlarged encounter with the divine.

Two great energies, or dynamic principles, drive the universe. The first is Eros, whom the Greeks considered a god. Paradoxically, Eros was the first of the gods and the last of the gods, perhaps because he is found at the origin of all things and is ever renewing himself in each new situation. Eros is the energy which seeks connection. Freud was right in suggesting that the world is erotic, for it is forever seeking to combine in new ways with the Other, whether at the molecular level or through the *Sehnsucht für Ewigekeit*. The other great power is Logos, the dividing power, the principle of development through differentiation. Its goal is clarity, or consciousness. When eros and logos combine, there is a synergy which is extraordinarily powerful. I often find such synergy in the writing of Rilke. His themes are the universal themes: love and death, what depth may be seen through simple things, and why we may be here on this spinning globe. For all the simplicity of subject, however, few writers have managed to point beyond the subject toward the numinous as profoundly as Rilke has.

For our purposes I need to restrict our consideration to two of the *Duino Elegies*. The ten *Duino Elegies* are verbal equivalents to Beethoven's nine symphonies; they derive their name from the Duino Castle on the Adriatic where, in 1912, Rilke was overtaken by a numinous voice which dictated the first line of the first elegy. He wrote the *Elegies* off and on for the next few years before publishing them together in 1923. The last elegies were completed in a paroxysm of creative spontaneity in 1922, and Rilke wrote a friend of his, "though I can barely manage to hold the pen, after several days of huge obedience to the spirit . . . I have climbed the mountain! At last! The Elegies are here, they exist."[2]

"Huge obedience to the spirit"—those are Rilke's own words for what is surely religious experience, the possession by the daimon who is both personal and universal, terrible and transformative. His obedience to this spirit is the necessary humility before the numinous—"Not my will but Thine"—and, like the mother's delivery of a child, occurs in revelatory suffering. Without suffering nothing genuinely new will come forth. Like Jacob wrestling with the angel, the courageous artist says "unless you bless me, I will not let go of you."

If we are honest with ourselves, we are obliged to admit that there was no significant psychological or spiritual growth in our life without the experience of suffering. This is why Jung defined neurosis as suffering which has not yet found its meaning, not that suffering could be eliminated. Moreover, in that form of religious expression which we find in aesthetic achievement, we acknowledge Orpheus as the mythic paradigm, the singer who descends into the underworld even as we descend into the unconscious to risk all—possibly to return with Euridice, or the golden bough, the new insight, or possibly to perish. All of these *catabases* and *anabases* require risk and suffering. The Danish theologian Søren Kierkegaard spoke of this paradox of the aesthetics of suffering, and the suffering of aesthetics, in a rather horrifying parable:

> A poet is an unhappy being whose heart is torn by secret sufferings, but whose lips are so strangely formed that when the sighs and cries escape them, they sound like beautiful music. His fate is like that of the unfortunate victims whom the tyrant Phalaris imprisoned in a brazen bull, and slowly tortured over a steady fire; their cries could not reach the tyrant's ears so as to strike terror into his heart: when they reached his ears they sounded like sweet music. And men crowd about the poet and say to him: "You must sing for us again soon." Which is as much to say, "May fresh sufferings torture your soul but may your lips be formed as before; for the cries would only frighten us, but the music is delicious."[3]

The theme of Rilke's two elegies on which we will focus are, quite simply, love and death, the old *Liebestod*, in whose grip Rilke strains to express the inexpressible, as Wagner does in the music of *Tristan und Isolde*.

What Do We Love When We Love?

Rilke's third elegy, written in 1912–13, explores the multilevels of intimate relationship. In relationship we move not only with conscious intention but in concert with deeper, more ancient motions, chthonic motives, primal forces, and telluric patterns. Rilke invokes the long tradition of *amor*, that powerful energy rescued by the troubadours and *Minnesingers* of the Middle Ages, that energy somewhere between eros and agape—personal, intimate, and universal at once.

It is one thing to sing of the Beloved. And another, alas, to invoke the secret, guilty River-God of the Blood.[4]

As we know more and more of the biological determinants in our lives, such as those affecting longevity or proclivity to certain illnesses and emotional states, so we recognize that our instinctual programming is profound, urgent, and insistent. Beneath the conventions of the praise of the beloved there are the older, darker forces—the wonderfully epithetic "River-God of the Blood." Such a force is personified and deified, and rightly so, for our encounter with such power is always archetypal, always capable of seizing us, possessing us, and carrying us along its canalized course. If it is guilty, then of what? The River-God is guilty in the sense that it secretly possesses us and obliges us to serve more than one motive in any relationship. It is this same chthonic power which creates *Liebeswahn*, or the love-madness in honor of the mad god who possesses souls and makes them insane in turn. Like the intimation of "lightening" in the name and nature of Zeus, so this duplicitous, hermetic god is always present.

Just as the inscription which Jung carved over the entrance to his home in Küsnacht reads, "Called or not called, God will be there," so Rilke acknowledges that conscious or unconscious as the lovers may be, the deeper and darker powers are immanent. Such an overpowering experience, which we characterize as love, is religious in character, given its *gravitas*, its compelling power, and its autonomy. We recall also Jung calling "god" that which crossed his path and overthrew his will for good or ill. Each of us has been in the hands of this god and has been swept along by its urgent flow.

What do these lovers know of "this lord of desire ... embodying the unknown" and "arousing the night to an endless clamor"? What can the thin wafer of consciousness know of the vast sea upon which it tosses? Each of us has a profound ambivalence toward the inner sea in which we swim. When James Joyce brought his schizophrenic daughter to Jung for a consultation, Jung replied, "She is drowning in that sea in which you learned to swim."[5] The sea of which he spoke was of course that oceanic world that each of us carries within, in which even our biographies toss in tumult.

Who of us has not been some latter-day Jonah, fleeing the summons to witness, being swallowed by the darksome, devouring sea-monster, and then being flung back upon an alien shore and obliged to reflect?

Like the "sinners in the hands of an angry God" of Jonathan Edwards, lovers are but frail and fragile wafers, bravely but naively set upon the sea.[6] And what telluric powers await such mariners? "Oh the Neptune of the blood, with his fearsome trident." We know the power of Poseidon/Neptune to shake us, drown us, wash us from the shore. We resonate to this archaic force with its terrible trident, whose skewers, like Cupid's arrows, sweetly wound and bring anguish into the world. "Oh the dark wind from his breast of spiraled shell." Thus the evocation not only of that pagan power but also the dark wind which emanates from him, the devouring *pneuma,* both wind and spirit, which animates, moves, carries away, and sometimes destroys. While the strategy of consciousness and of convention is to appeal to the stars, "the primal constellations," to some celestial setting to summon up the image of the beloved, Rilke reminds us that we are in the hands of the river-god, the nihilistic Neptune with his terrible trident. Beware those who love passionately, then, for they are taken and tossed, and often lost.

Rilke did not read Jung to the best of my knowledge, but as a deeply perceptive and intuitive individual he mined the same regions of the psyche. He knows that something larger than consciousness is evoked, that the dark river god courses from a chthonic place. Beyond and below the beloved, Rilke intuits the parental imago. The beloved only stirs the memories, the paradigm, the programmed imago of the Intimate Other. Speaking to the beloved he says, "Truly you did shake his heart with older terrors, rippled through him in deeper shocks. Call him, but you cannot pull him away from a deeper intercourse."

The "deeper intercourse" to which Rilke alludes consists of those first and primal relationships, the internalization of which creates a profound sense of Self and Other, and of the transactions between them. All of our lives these primal parental imagoes are transferred to ever new relationships, and their tyranny is all the greater when they are unconscious. As Shakespeare observed in *The Tempest,* no prisons are more confining than the ones of which we are unaware.

The child's internalization of his or her mother becomes the template which all other relationships replicate or struggle to transcend. It sounds terribly reductionistic to us, deterministic even, to speak of such profound and pervasive influence, but if one looks long enough, and deeply enough, one finds always the trace of the parent-child dyad informing the choice, strategies, and often outcomes of later relationships. Even the compensatory fantasy that one is choosing the opposite of one's parental imago still shows one to be defined by the original experience. How much of ourselves do we ever choose? Rilke raises the same question.

> *But did he begin himself?*
> *Mother, you made his small self;*
> *For you he was new . . .*
> *And you bestowed on him friendly eyes,*
> *and protected him from things foreign.*

One could offer an *ad hominem* analysis of Rilke's emphasis on the power of this primal, maternal matrix, and indeed, he did suffer from a powerfully negative mother complex. On a separate occasion he wrote,

> *Ah, woe is me, my mother rends me.*
> *Then I put stone upon stone around me*
> *And stood there like a little house,*
> *Around which day moved magnificently,*
> *Ever alone.*
> *Now comes my mother, comes and rends me.*

Although Rilke once confessed that he did not love his mother, his treatment of the mother in the third elegy is benign, even laudatory. And he is not wrong in his assertion of this primal power of the mother, for she is the immediate, immanent experience of life and of relationship, for good or ill, and she is the mediator with the larger world outside. As an analyst, I am obliged to agree with his conclusion that the power of the mother experience, for men and for women, is, generally speaking, the single greatest psychological influence in our lives.

The mother depicted in this elegy is protective rather than devouring. When the child's room is full of shadows and sounds at night and his terror rises to fill that vast space, which "you made harmless." He writes that "there wasn't a night-noise your smile could not assuage, as if your omniscience had already known such sounds."

As the mediatrix with the world, the mother's fears, unlived life, and projected desires become part of the internal mythology of the child. His or her conduct of adult life, psychology, theology, and relationships will all seek either to confirm, to compensate for, or to heal the mythologems implicit in this first, primal relationship. Jung agreed that Freud's Oedipal complex was universal but had as its motive not sexual congress but immersion in the all-protective, all-nurturing source, against which only the hero's journey could overthrow the seductive power of such satiety. As Jung explains, the child "tears himself away from the mother, from the domestic hearth, to rise through battle to his destined heights. Always he imagines his worst enemy in front of him, yet he carries the enemy within himself—a deadly longing for the abyss, a longing to drown in his own source, to be sucked down into the realm of the Mothers."[7]

No doubt Rilke used his transcendent aesthetic powers to escape that devouring mother, but she was forever present in his intimate relationships. That wise American poet Walt Whitman must have had a similar feeling when he wrote of a "Dark Mother" that always followed him.

Rilke acknowledges this awesome mediatorial and directive power: "So tenderly powerful your presence as you stood by the bed, that his Fate slid behind the wardrobe, and his stirring Future slipped into the folds of the curtains."

Rilke's testimony to the power of such primal experience may seem overstated to some. In both men and women, however, the deeply buried imprint of such experience constitutes a de facto mythology, by which I mean a weltanschauung, a set of values, an assemblage of behaviors and attitudes, and a propulsive power for reenactment. All subsequent relationships begin in projection, move toward the transference of such implicit mythologies, and unconsciously seek to replicate, compensate for, or heal the first relationship. Anyone who works analytically will find this core truth in the heart of any serious analysis.

The internalization of the personal mother constitutes the personal dimension, or what Jung called the "mother complex" of the child. The word *complex* here is entirely neutral. It simply means the internalization of a powerful experience which, affectively charged, has the capacity to act autonomously when activated and, given its origin in the past, tends to create repetitions—patterns based on the dynamics of its origin. We know how difficult it is simply to be in *this* moment, for this moment is reflexively compared with other such moments, and the psychic history of the person is dynamically present and invasive. Only when we respond spontaneously or instinctually to an event are we in the moment; most of the time, we are in history, for history is dynamically within us. To think otherwise is the insidious ploy of the ego to serve its fantasy of control.

Most women will testify that their male partners often engage with them as they would their mother, seeking to please them, to control them, or to avoid them. Men cannot help but have the mother imago activated when in the presence of intimate relationship. And the power which the mother held in his life floods him, unconsciously, and sets in motion the protective motives which confound his partner. He does not think of her as his mother, but the historically generated complex is blind to the present and floods this moment with the mythologems of origins.

Yet even the personal mother is as a fragment floating on a vast sea. Without knowing anything of Jung's conceptualization of the collective unconscious, Rilke intuits that we all are moved by formative forces which lie beneath personal history. Jung spoke of the longing to be sucked down into "the realm of the Mothers." His capitalization of the maternal bespeaks more an archetypal imago than personal complex. As the child sleeps, under the embracing care of his Mother, Rilke continues, "he seemed protected . . . but inside who could divert the ancestral floods within him?"

Inside him, "the ancestral floods." What floods, what origin? What secret sources antedate the personal mother who has been the pervasive presence from the moment of his birth? Jung suggested that every complex has its archetypal root reaching down into our prehistories. In each affectively charged complex, which is a personal experience, there is a substratum—our instinctual, animal nature, which is inherited by the species and is our grounding in the Great Mother archetype. In this most transient condition of mortality there are webs of programmed tissues and autonomous energies which move us to rhythms not consciously ours. Who or what invents our dreams, our religions, our patterned choices? What powers move us to reproduce, to build civilization, to long for meaning? These are the gods, namely, the archetypal powers which are more ancient than we can imagine. These powers shape us. As Rilke continues, "he was subsumed, enmeshed, in the spreading web of inner events, with paradigms of vegetal and animal forms."

We all know those "vegetal and animal forms" and have always known them. They were more immediate to us when we were children. We knew they lived, for they stalked our dreams and were glimpsed in our nursery rhymes and bedtime stories. But we learned to distance them and build the protective walls of ego to defend ourselves against them. Occasionally the poet will remind us of these animal forms, whether outer or inner, as Yeats does in his poem "Nineteen Hundred and Nineteen": "Now days are dragon-ridden, the nightmare / Rides upon sleep."[8]

Still, these abysses are not just terrifying; they are also our home. We come thence, and we carry such unconscious chasms wherever we go. Rilke imagines as well that the child can love this world within, embrace it, and be one with his nature: "Oh how he gave himself over— loved his inner wilderness, the primal wood, amid whose density his heart stood light-green."

His heart is light and green, the color of the Great Mother, and light-green, for it rests lightly in the bosom of its true home. Again, we see the personification of the archetypal imagination which allows us momentary access to such mysteries. These divine powers cannot be named or contained, but they can be apprehended by virtue of the mediating symbol.

When one is in the presence of this archetypal field, one is full of terror like the biblical prophet who fears the Lord. But this fear is more accurately awe. Existentialism reminds us that the abyss is our home, and our freedom is found in embracing that abyss which we also carry within. Rilke imagines that the child, when one with his own nature, leaves "his ancestral roots, and goes out into the primal source where his tiny birth was already transcended."

The child we were, the child we carry still, is the carrier of ancient energies. Recall that it is the energy which is real, not the husk which holds it for a time and then releases it to seek other incarnations. The source to which Rilke alludes may be called God or nature or, more adequately, the Mystery, but we are its carriers. This little incarnation we call our lives is but the vehicle for a larger journey which divinity makes through us. Jung's idea of individuation is not in service to the narcissistic inflation of the ego; it is a humbling assumption of the task which fate has assigned to us. We are asked to become the individual in order that our small portion of the unfolding of the divine may be achieved. To flag or fail in that task is to injure God.

So, in his natural, instinctual self, the child is comfortable with those deep places where later ego will fear to tread. Rilke describes this descent into our own nature: "Lovingly, he descends into the ancestral blood, to canyons where the Frightful may be found, turgid with Fathers, where even Terror knew him, winked at him."

Several matters of note are found here. Drawn by love, the unfettered eros of nature naturing, becoming itself, the child visits the places where, according to my translation, he swims in the primal blood, where the feared presence is faced and is no longer feared. Once in Zurich, just before I spent my first internship on a locked psychiatric ward, I expressed my beginner's apprehension. My analyst replied, "When you have faced your terrors, the demons of others won't terrify you." Immediately I knew the wisdom of his remark and realized I feared less the violence there than the loss of the tether to comfortable sanity. If I could let go of that tether, I would be able to be present to those "animal forms" that haunted the patients and treat them as familiar.

One puzzling note arises with Rilke's depiction of the primal ravine as glutted with the fathers. This puzzle may be his acknowledgment of the inaccessibility of the father energy to help him compensate for the power of that devouring mother, or it may be that the "fathers" here represent the telluric powers of old Chronos, generative but destructive, and in time plowed under as well. Time is unkindly even to gods.

We take special note of how the Fearful seems to know the youth, and winks at him. We recall that the etymology of _numinous_ suggests something which is nodding toward us—something that seeks us, knows us, solicits our mindfulness, and invites our complicity. How many times have we had dream figures whom we do not know consciously but feel we somehow know, or those anonymous figures who seem to know us? We recall Jung's subjective, synthetic approach to dreams and his idea that the various parts of the dream, the personified energies, are parts of us. We are led to conclude that there is some superordinate reality, what Jung called the Self, which knows us, creates the dream, and synthesizes so many disparate elements into a dramatic whole. When we are in the presence of that large wisdom, such as when we revere and dialogue with our dreams, we are in the presence of the transcendent whose name and nature are unknown but whose reality is palpable. Who could doubt the presence of the gods when one has been vouchsafed visions of eternity through the lineaments of the literal? Or as Rilke muses, "Why should he not love what looked lovingly at him?"

How could we not love that which nods at us and beckons us to be restored to wholeness? Even before his mother, he had loved this world, this cosmos from which he sprung, "long before, while you carried him in the womb, that dissolved the cosmos, which wafted the embryo so lightly."

Surely the deepest wound of this world we inhabit is to feel uprooted from our divine beginning. It is one thing to wander as a hungry spirit, as we do; it is something worse to have forgotten that we carry the sacred energy within us, and are present to it, wheresoever we are. As transient beings we are nonetheless the carriers of the eternal. How powerful is Rilke's endorsement of this journey: "See, we do not love as the flowers do, for a single year, for a timeless liquor flows through our arms."

As hackneyed as the word *love* is, as jaded as the word *God* or the phrase "have a nice day," we are still obliged to use them. What Rilke is calling love is surely the toughest, most resilient energy in the cosmos, the energy which survives and is manifest in endlessly diverse ways to all the senses. This love is the eros which seeks connection, the desire which drives life in the face of the seductive terrors of the abyss. We err to think such a force reserved for only one person, our magical partner, our erotic *Doppelgänger*. It is expended as well on "seething multitudes" and "the fathers lying in our depths." All of this ancient drama has preceded the *pas de deux* we call love, which our culture is driven to both venerate and narrow to mere venery or sexual indulgence because it knows itself impoverished by the loss of the gods.

Thus, the beloved is the recipient, certainly, of powerful energies, but how would she have surmised "what archaic hours you stir in your lover" or "what feelings arise out of ancient being"? How deeply moved would we be if we were to perceive such an ancient drama not only in us but in the other as well? How much more could we love them if we saw the invisible histories that moved in and through them? How could we then lead them "nearer to Eden," that place of beginnings, departures, losses, and wistful reminiscences? What could we see in the other, what mystery, what worthy history, would open up the glottal stops of our hearts and allow us to bestow on them that which "vanquishes the heavy nights"?

With Rilke we see the fine fusion of eros and logos, the deep yearning to connect with the delicate differentiation of language to summon, to intimate, but not to define or close off. When we gloss this poem, as I have, we have not understood it, or contained it, for it continues to own us and remains elusive. One does not contain the divine. It manifests, abides a while, and departs, leaving but a trace, through the artifacts of consciousness which sought to retain and possess it.

In this third elegy Rilke has summoned the highest, most mysterious energies, which we often subsume under the appellation *love*. As Eros was a god, he was not to be defined. He nods at us, moves through us, and then, at his whim, leaves us. He is not to be restrained, for he is of the godly ones. Rilke's gift is to bring us to a place where Eros is glimpsed, along with all the declivities in which he abides. We cannot remain, but it is a great gift to have been afforded a moment there.

Why Are We Sojourners on This Earth?

In the ninth of his *Duino Elegies,* begun in 1912 but not concluded until 1922, the year of Eliot's "The Waste Land," Rilke asks another immense question, namely, why are we here on this spinning earth?

The magnificent ninth elegy begins with the question, "Why?" Why in this interlude of grace which we call our lives are we human? Human beings, doomed to die, are cursed and/or blessed with consciousness, yet cling fervently to their mortal fates. The word *Frist* often suggests the notion of "grace," even in the ordinary sense of a grace period, a moment of granted time. Grace we know is something given, something lent, not something earned. Dylan Thomas alluded to the same gift of time in his famous poem "Fern Hill," where he notes that Time allows us but "a few tuneful turnings / before the children, green and golden, follow him out of grace."[9] So we are here only a fleeting moment, graced by the gods, given consciousness (Promethean burden as that is), yearning for love and for union, and tasked with limited powers to transcend a certain fate. Why, then, are we here?

Not for happiness, Rilke concludes, which itself is so fleeting, so uncertain, so unretainable. Nor for simple curiosity, though such has led us to the depths of the oceans, to interstellar space, and to the exploration of our own labyrinthian minds. Nor simply as discipline for the heart, for we know that the heart may grow sated, break in pain, and prove as much the agent of trickery as our cunning and divided minds.

Rilke comes to a stunning conclusion. We are here because "this fleeting world" apparently *needs* us, we who are paradoxically, "the most fleeting of all." Each of us is here to observe, to bear witness to all things, if only once, and no more. This, our condition, too, is our task.

And we, also, only once. And never again. But to have been here *once,* if only for this *once,* to have been on this earth *once,* seems immutable.[10]

We are here, he suggests, to complete some purpose in the cosmos, a purpose which has nothing to do with our own will or hybris. We are here to help creation by being the agent of its consciousness. This is an idea that Jung also reached via a quite different route. In his controversial work *Answer to Job,* Jung argued that Yahweh needed humans to carry the task of His consciousness, His conscience, and His own evolution.[11] At first glance Jung's argument sounds preposterous, certainly anthropocentric, and hybristic. Moreover, Jung's argumentative acumen in *Answer to Job* would make a believer squirm. He shows the contradictions in Yahweh's own statements; he demonstrates the lack of moral development of those positions; and he cries out on behalf of human suffering and injustice in questioning whether such a deity is worthy of worship. Jung was no fool and later indicated that he wished he had changed every reference to God to the *god-imago.* He knew well enough to leave the arguments for God to the philosophers of religion and the credos to persons of faith. He was more interested in showing the evolution of human consciousness, which is what he meant by the evolving god-imago. The *imago Dei,* he argued, tells us much about an individual or a culture and very little about the Wholly Other.

Rilke is no fool either, and he asserts that our *raison d'être* lies in our capacity for growth as agents of consciousness. By each person becoming more conscious, the cosmos gains consciousness.

But the capacity for consciousness is no sure thing. Of what, really, can we become conscious? Isolated facts here and there, occasional patterns, and rarely, deep intimations of the divine through dreams, visions, art, and mythologies. We keep trying to catch and hold what seems so fleeting, "we try to possess, to hold lightly in our simple hands, with our stupefied gaze, our tongueless heart. Wishing to become it, yet to whom may we pass it on? Though we long to hold on to it forever."

Our brains are feeble tools in the face of complexity and immensity. Our sight is sated, our hearts rendered dumb and inarticulate. We wish to merge with the flow, to become it, and it passes by us. And what are we to do with what we perceive, to whom do we give it, that which we can so scarcely retain? Without the tools of metaphor and symbol we would have precious little to say, for they allow us to talk about that about which we cannot talk.

And what can be taken with us into the darker kingdom? What survives us? We cannot, Rilke asserts, take with us what we saw. We can take nothing which we have achieved here. What golden bough do we have to allow us to visit that darker kingdom and return? We carry the long lessons of love, the capacity to care about something or someone, but even that may pass, and certainly the spinning planets and stately stars are fixed in their orbits whether we raise a tumult or pass quietly into nothingness. (Recall Edward Hirsch's lines cited earlier, "Stars are the white tears of nothingness. / Nothingness grieves over the disintegrating gods.")

Perhaps our place or vocation here is not unlike that of the mountain traveler who returns to the valley and speaks the name of some new flower seen, some gentian to bring as a souvenir and talisman of the ascent taken. But the key here, Rilke says, is in the *saying*. Here he echoes the Hebrew imagination in Genesis which analogizes the mystery of creativity in God's capacity to speak. With the word spoken, the thing arises out of chaos into being: "perhaps we are here in order to *speak*, to pronounce *house, bridge, fountain, gate, pitcher, fruit-tree, window*—at most *column, tower*. But to *speak*, understand, oh to *speak* more intensely than the things themselves could ever attain."

Our task is formidable and simple: to bear witness, to assist into being, to help house, bridge, fountain, gate, pitcher, and so on exist more intensely than they would without us. In a letter written in 1925, Rilke noted, "Even for our grandparents a 'house,' a 'well,' a familiar tower, their very clothes, their coat, was infinitely more intimate; almost everything was a vessel in which they found what is human and added to the supply of what is human."[12] To add to the supply of what is human is our deepest destiny, which, amid death and transience, brings joy. Here Rilke's exclamatory joy is contained in the *O zu sagen*, "Oh to *speak!*" What joy! Here Rilke echoes the secondary imagination of which Coleridge wrote, the echo of the primal "I Am that I Am" of Yahweh. Here we are co-creators with the Creator—humble servants, but partners in creation itself. What a *vocatus!*

We who are most fleeting are summoned, nonetheless, to this calling, a calling which transpires only in the passing moment but exists for that moment. Perhaps the finest love poem I have ever seen was written by Archibald MacLeish and takes its title and its cue from one of Shakespeare's sonnets, "Not Marble Nor Gilded Monuments." Shakespeare, writing to his beloved, "the dark ladie" of the sonnets, which were written at the time of plague in London, expresses the hope that the immortality of his writing will grant continued life for these two mortal lovers. MacLeish denies that his writing will grant any immortality to himself or the beloved.

I will not speak of the famous beauty of dead women.
I will say the shape of a leaf lay once on your hair.
Till the world ends and the eyes are out and the
       mouths broken,
Look! it is there![13]

For MacLeish the recognition utterance, more exclamation than description, bestows meaning on that existential moment and grants it deepened being. For MacLeish, for Rilke, as for classical Buddhism, the past is past and the future is not yet. Only this moment exists. As Rilke exclaims, "Here is the speakable moment; here is its home. Speak and bear witness. While the Things themselves are slipping away more than ever."

Rilke capitalizes *Things,* not just because all nouns are capitalized in German but because he wants to accord the things of our world—the house, bridge, fountain, gate—mutual being and to celebrate that being. We know even more than Rilke did of how evanescent the things around us are. We live in a plastic, throwaway culture, a culture based on momentary sensation and transient tastes. How much more important for us, then, than in 1920, to affirm, to render what is real amidst the fleeting moments and disappearing things. Through this affirmation we come at last to Rilke's vision of why we are here. Put simply, through the acts of consciousness, reverence, mindfulness, and speech, we are here to *praise.* We, the most fleeting, bring meaning into the world through the verbal venues of praise.

> Between hammers, our heart persists, as does the tongue between
> our teeth and still, persisting, praises.

Our *vocatus* is to praise and, by doing so, grant things deeper being and bring consciousness to them. This is very consistent with Jung's idea of the place of consciousness and our task here.

In Jung's view, humanity is a partner in the continuing incarnation of Being. Being springs forth from the Mystery, from inexplicable cosmic energies—who among us can understand the miraculous nature of everyday life, or of a baby, or of the quantum dynamics of the atom? But through the act of consciousness, mindfulness, or what Rilke calls praise, we bring meaning to those transient moments. As Jung writes, "As far as we can discern, the sole purpose of human existence is to kindle a light in the darkness of mere being." He also writes of that partnership with the Divine which brings our spiritual task: "The myth of the necessary incarnation of God . . . can be understood as man's creative confrontation with the opposites and their synthesis in the self, the wholeness of his personality . . . That is the goal . . . which fits man meaningfully into the scheme of creation and at the same time confers meaning upon it."[14]

Jung's use of the idea of myth is clear enough as an expression of dramatically rendered values which activate and direct the energies of the soul, but such a phrase as "the necessary incarnation of God" may strike us as strange. The name and nature of the Divine remain shrouded in mystery, of course, and we may only glimpse the invisible when it momentarily inhabits the visible world. What passes unnoticed is not unreal, but it depends on human consciousness to bring it full identity. To this partnership with the invisible world we bring recognition. The Mystery confers being, but the human *saying* confers meaning. The world does not *mean;* it *is.* We are the organisms of meaning and make our contribution through the gift of consciousness.

Rilke could have stopped the ninth elegy with this superlative insight, but he goes further. Throughout the *Duino Elegies* he invokes an angel, in the same way in which Milton invoked the "heavenly muse" or Plato, the daimon. Rilke asks us to "praise this world to the angel." We are asked to bring praise to the cosmos. We cannot bring the gift of understanding, for there is much which eludes our petty intelligence, nor can we bring only large emotion, for there is much which exceeds our capacity. Rather we are asked to tell the angel of the simple places and sights we have seen, to speak of "the rope-maker in Rome or the potter along the Nile," to show "how blessed the Thing can be, and how guileless." These unremarkable events are most remarkable, for they summon mere Things up and out of the flux into consciousness, wherein they take on enlarged destiny. Remember, Rilke has argued that these transient Things need us for deeper being than they are otherwise capable: "And these transient Things know you are praising them. They, most fleeting, look to us, the most fleeting of all, for redemption."

In this paradox of being, with the transience of all things, the soul longs for permanence. However momentary this life we lead, Rilke and Jung suggest that the vocation of naming, of praising, of becoming conscious plays an immense role in the unfolding of the cosmos. These things around us look to us for deliverance from obscurity, from obloquy, from oblivion.

Like the ascending tones of Wagner's "Liebestod," which stretch toward eternity, Rilke takes this task one step further in his conclusion. Our sacred vocation is to redeem the earth: "Earth, is this not what you desire, invisibly . . . ? Is not transformation your most urgent yearning?"

The transformation of the earth comes from the engagement with consciousness whereby the mysterious stuff of life is given a spiritual identity through the experience of meaning. Our participation in this partnership is homeopathic, for underneath material appearances, the same divine energies course through us. That energy brings life, to which our consciousness brings meaning.

Yet we and the earth are part of a single reality. And speaking to this ever-evolving earth, Rilke says: "Oh believe me, you do not need your Springtimes to vanquish me again, for one, only one surfeits the blood. Namelessly, from the beginning, I have been yours. You are always right, and your deepest truth is intimate Death."

We can imagine a springtime, with the thrust of life from the heavy earth, but can we imagine no observant consciousness to praise it? We know what it means to drive through the spring countryside and see the red and blue bursts of wildflowers. They will be there with or without us, but it was our consciousness which named them Indian paintbrush and bluebonnets.

But Rilke turns the matter one step further in suggesting that death is a holy inspiration and our most intimate companion. Precisely because our moments are few and finite, precisely because consciousness is so easily annihilated, the moments of meaning which we bring to this place are all the more precious. It is death which makes meaning possible, for without it there would be only endless repetition and meaningless choice. With mortality, choice takes on significance and we are obliged to discern what matters. In a letter written in 1923 Rilke clarifies,

I am not saying that we should *love* death; but we should love life so generously, so without calculation and selection, that we involuntarily come to include, and to love death too. . . . Only because we exclude death, when it suddenly enters our thoughts, has it become more and more a stranger to us; and because we have kept it a stranger, it has become our enemy. . . . [Death is] our friend precisely when we most passionately, most vehemently, assent to being here, to living and working on earth, to Nature, to love.[15]

From Greek mythology we recall Tithonus, who was granted immortality, found it a boring burden, and went to the gods to plead that his mortality might be restored. As a blessing, they granted him the power to die and, with that power, the capacity, indeed, the necessity for, meaning. So Death, which accompanies the baby's cry, which stands watching at our side, and whose imperatives none can deny, requires us to become conscious, to become creatures of choice. *We have been granted mortality that we might have meaning, and have it abundantly.*

Rilke concludes this mighty ninth symphony of praise by affirming the power of *this* moment, this radical experience of presence. "Look, I am living!" he exclaims. Not out of the childhood past, nor the future which may or may not be, but out of this moment. Just as MacLeish wrote that "the shape of a leaf lay in your hair . . . Look! it is there!", so Rilke celebrates this moment where "overwhelming Being floods my heart." This moment, this fleeting moment, is so full, and the more so because it is fleeting. This fate we have, to be mortal beings and to be conscious of that mortality, also begets our destiny, which is to bring meaning into the world, to create a life and a sensibility for which only the word *praise* may suffice.

On the Naming of the Gods[16]

Unlike so much of modern psychology, which has abrogated its immense responsibility to be present to the large issues of soul and meaning and which has reduced humanity to behaviors, cognitions, and biochemical drives, Rilke and Jung dared to address the large questions.

What can be larger for us than love, death, and the divine? We see that Jung and Rilke approach such mysteries with reverence, a desire to know, an awareness of limitations, and, fortunately, with a huge imaginative power. To turn away from these large concerns is the failure of nerve; to take them on is what restores us to our dignity and our destiny.

The task of the poet, and the depth psychologist, is to bring us into proximity with the sacred. The sacred is only knowable through experience and then made meaningful and communicated by the agencies of metaphor and symbol. Sometimes the sacred is remarkable for its absence, sometimes for its anarchic quality, sometimes for its presence beneath the surface of ordinary experience. For Rilke the naming of "house," "tree," and "fountain," was a holy event if sensibility was open to depth. There are lines by the German poet Friedrich Hölderlin, whom Jung frequently cited: "God is near but difficult to grasp, but where danger lies, from there, too, deliverance emerges."[17] And it is that paradox that St. Augustine confessed where we, "unlovely," rush "heedlessly among the things of beauty," where the divine is with us, but we are not with the divine.[18] It is the time of the Great In-Between, the space between Words. As Heidegger describes this spiritual interregnum of modernism: "It is the time of the gods that have fled and of the god that is coming. It is the time of need, because it lies under a double lack and a double Not: the No-more of the gods that have fled and the Not-yet of the god that is coming."[19]

Poetry is not affectation then, nor aesthetic sleight of hand, but a mediation between humanity and the numinous. Jung makes the poet's contribution clear: "Poets are the first in their time to divine the darkly moving, mysterious currents, and to express them according to the limits of their capacity in more or less speaking symbols. They make known, like true prophets, the deep motions of the collective unconscious, 'the will of God' . . . which, in the course of time, must inevitably come to the surface as a general phenomenon."[20]

Just as the dream synthesizes materials unknown to consciousness, and the intuitive function accesses dimensions of reality beyond thought and sensation, so the poetic sensibility discerns the deepest need and brings forth images to speak the unspeakable, and to render the invisible world accessible.

Reference to a few of Rilke's shorter poems may illustrate this capacity of the archetypal imagination to "name the gods" by providing images which link us once again to the numinous.

I Find You in All These Things

I find You in all these things,
to which I am a brother in all,
in which minuscule seed you minutely hide yourself
and in the Great, you greatly reveal yourself.

This wondrous game of power
which unfolds itself in submission:
stretching through the roots, thickening in the trunks,
and resurrecting through the treetops.[21]

In the original Rilke uses the lowercase *dich* (you rather than You), and though one may translate that word as *Lord,* Rilke may be even more subtle. He does not name this god directly, though we sense the godly coursing through nature. All things pulse with this life; in the dormant seed the divine sleeps; and through the vastness the Vast reveals itself. In this manifestation of power Rilke finds the paradox of submission. The highest is found in the lowest root, and he distantly alludes to the submission of Christ on the tree of Golgotha, the humble servant who rises from the dead.

While Rilke could not personally express a Christian credo, he could appeal to that tradition and certainly did evoke the archetypal pattern of the vegetative god which runs through Adonis to Tammuz to Osiris to Dionysus to Christ. Under the weight of institutions, under the encrustation of dogma and ritual, Rilke recovers wonder and reinstitutes the wisdom of Hermes Trismegistus: that things above are copies of things below and through the archetypal image the gods bring the timeless into our time.

Rilke lived in the time between the no-more and the not-yet. As a poet he knew that we always live in the space between words, but as a modern he also knew that we live in the space between Words. His poem

"Lament" expresses the sense of loss and the pathos of longing which we all feel: "Everything is far and long gone by. I think that the star glittering above me has been dead for a million years."[22]

The transient things of our lives have left us: places, friends, loved ones. Upon what do we place our faith, from what metaphysical benchmark may we find our place, chart our course? Even the star above us has long ago blinked off and the distance is so vast the news has not yet reached us. It is noteworthy that our word *desire* refers to the mariner's star by which a course is charted. The loss of the guiding star means we are unable to find the shore we seek. Rilke says that he would like to "step out of my heart," but he cannot sacrifice his spiritual pain lest he lose who he is in the process. He says he "would like to pray," but to whom? As he looks through the vast night with all its dark holes waiting to suck us in, he nonetheless believes that one of those stars still flames alive. He concludes: "I believe I know which one alone endures, which one, at the end of its rays, still stands like a White City."[23]

What a wonderful rendering of the modernist condition—the sense of a past unretrievable, a future unimaginable, and the need to continue one's journey without guidance. What a wonderful summons to the existential risk and trust in the supportive cosmos in his evocation of that white city which stands, still, at the end of its infinitely long beam.

In the lyric "Autumn," Rilke nominates not only a season of the soil but a season of the soul as well. This seems fitting, since we live in the waning days of some large history but cannot yet glimpse the rebirth which will spring forth later. He analogizes the falling autumnal leaves with the fading of distant gardens in the sky. The loss is Edenic, taking from us not only the recent summer but also the fabled garden of innocence. And through the cosmic night the earth, too, is falling:

> *All of us are falling. See this hand now fall.*
> *And now see the others; it is part of all.*
>
> *And still there is one who in his hands gently*
> *Holds this falling endlessly.*[24]

Notice that Rilke does not name this god. It is not Baal, or Yahweh, or any of the million deities which have been reified and have disappeared from this planet. He anthropomorphizes this power through the image of gentle hands, hands which hold us eternally, even as we fall through time and space. Naming the god is to define and control it. Rilke is a most religious poet for he is able to evoke the divine, intimate the numinous, and yet allow it to remain as it is—mysterious, elusive, Other.

And for the last example, I turn to the poem which expresses its thesis in its first line: "Now is the time when the Gods emerge / from occupied Things."[25] As we have seen before, the Things of this world are not inanimate to the poet; each throbs with life and carries the imprint of the gods on its frail form. We recall Jung ascribing divinity to those events which crossed his path and violently overturned ego's intent, and Rilke asserts that they "overthrew every wall in my house."[26] It is often difficult to accept that the Divine Will may not be concordant with our own, that the path for which we are intended is not that which we would have chosen. I recall an analyst in Zurich asking which member of our small group had chosen to be there; no one replied. Who, he asked, had no choice but to be there, and all nodded assent.

Not only do we flee the disruptive powers of the gods, we tend to shun the invitation to enlargement which such encounters invite. In every visitation to the swamplands of the soul there is a task for the enlargement of consciousness, whether we will it or not. And Jung reminded us to flee these invitations at our peril. Oedipus, who was the smartest man in Thebes, knew not himself, and that of which he was unconscious led to the fulfillment of the oracles. "When an inner situation is not made conscious, it happens outside as fate," Jung writes. Elsewhere he argues that genuine encounters with the Self, or with the gods, as Rilke would have it, are usually suffered as defeats by the ego.[27]

Rilke evokes those gods, calls forth the unnameable ones: "Oh you Gods, who once came often, but now slumber in Things."[28]

For the animistic world of our ancestors, nature was charged with soul-stuff. The trees, the streams, the animal life was divinity itself, in all its manifold forms—fearful, joyous, always profound. In de-souling nature, we gained greater manipulation of the material world, but at the loss of meaningful relation to it. Rilke knows that the gods have not left; they have gone underground and wait to be resummoned from the world of Things: "Again it is your rebirth, Gods. We only repeat things. But you are the primal source. The world arises from you, and these beginnings glisten through the crevices of all our failures."[29]

The recovery of spirituality in our time will not likely come from the revivication of someone else's experience, for experience is seldom if ever transferred. It will come through our capacity to open to radical experience (from the word *radix,* or "root" experience), whether through our encounters with nature, each other, or the insurgencies of our own psyches. Rilke reminds us that the gods alone are the source of the renewal of meaning. Recall that we are using the word *gods* here to describe those images which rise spontaneously out of depth encounters. Whatever metaphysical status they may have is another question, but that they are psychologically compelling is irrefragable. Our failure is the failure of the imagination. Racism or bigotry is the failure of imagination, the power to image the world which the Other embodies. Our failure is to have traded the experience of the divine for the fantasy of control.

This decision, made centuries ago, and reinformed by most contemporary theologies and all ego-based psychologies, required the gods to go underground and remain within our unconscious, to emerge in projections, addictions, and sociopathies. But the gods are not dead. Nietzsche was, like Rilke, a man of radical faith when in the nineteenth century he announced the death of God. He cared enough about the questions of meaning to denounce the encapsulation of the gods in sterile rite and dogma. But he knew that the vitality of the divine was to be found elsewhere. He knew the truth of those lines of Yeats: "Whatever flames upon the night / Man's own resinous heart has fed."[30]

Through the powers of the archetypal imagination, allied with logos, which brings consciousness, such philosophers and poets have kept the gods alive by retaining a respectful humility before the Mystery, and by finding images whose power brings us into proximity with the numinous and compels a new encounter with the divine.

CHAPTER 3

Incarnational Imaginings

The Painter's Eye on Eternity

Primordial experiences rend from top to bottom the cur-
tain upon which is painted the picture of an ordered
world and allows a glimpse into the unfathomable abyss
of the unborn and of things yet to be. Is it a vision of
other worlds, or of the darkness of the spirit, or of the
primal beginnings of the human psyche?
—C. G. Jung

A Critical Place to Stand

What we wish most to know, most desire, remains unknowable and lies
beyond our grasp. The late-nineteenth-century art critic Walter Pater
once observed that all art aspires to the condition of music. I believe
he meant by this that music is an inherent, natural experience which
has no content per se, that is, denotated meaning, though it does have
form, rhythm, and progression. By aspiring to the condition of music,
art then transcends the tyranny of ideology, the popularity of an idea,
or the need to understand it. As that great American philosopher Louis
Armstrong once observed, if you have to have jazz explained to you,
you will never know what it means.

Nonetheless, in aspiring to the condition of music, the arts inevitably employ "language" that is generally referential, or connotative, and
motifs that are identifiable by consciousness. I should like to summarize briefly the perspectives and the pitfalls of any analysis of the arts.

ART AS IDEA

Many forms of art employ an idea, as we just saw in Rilke's contemplation of love and death. But we do not read a work of art to get a new idea. The idea of a novel or play will simply come down to a truism: "we love and are betrayed," or "we long for meaning," or "in the end we die." As Hemingway once observed, if the hero does not die in the end, the author simply did not finish the story. And what if the idea that fuels a work of art is one with which we disagree? Are we then to throw the entire work away? If one is not moved to ideological and affective compliance with medieval Catholicism, should Dante's *Commedia* be discarded? Surely there is more to a work of art than the idea which spawned it, an idea which may itself be commonplace, even in an original aesthetic expression.

ART AS FORM

I was educated in the era of the New Criticism, which argued that the idea of a work of art was essentially irrelevant and that the work manifests a series of structures, rhetorics, and agencies such as metaphor, symbol, or irony. The analysis of the work of art was essentially the analysis of the craft of art, irrespective of its cultural *Sitz im Leben* or its ideology. In these later days of deconstructionism we are told that the work of art is always a Rorschach reflection of its creator, inevitably revealing class, gender, and other biases. In neither approach to the arts do we find ourselves addressing why we are moved by art or how it deepens our journey.

ART AS RELATIONSHIP TO NATURE

As one examines the history of the arts, visual, literary, and musical, over the last two centuries, one sees a progressive decline in the importance of ideology for sure, but even more of a shift in our relationship to nature. Consider painting, for example. In the early nineteenth century Jacques Louis David might still be summoned to depict a historic event, such as the crowning of Napoleon. The Barbizon school certainly depicted the richness of nature, but one begins to see a loosening of the line and a growing fuzziness of color in those forests and fields. In Joseph Turner we see the anticipation of impressionism.

For the impressionists, the object is no longer paramount. Light is their subject, light as it is reflected and refracted from surfaces—water, lilies, colorful attire. Quickly they are followed by the expressionists, whose painting celebrated the emotions occasioned by their subjects; the pointillists, who see even the light as a series of luminous points; the cubists, who see constituent shapes only, interesting in and for themselves; the vorticists, who celebrate energy itself; and the abstract-ionists, in whose art the object disappears altogether. This history of modern art shows that *art progressively becomes the subject of art.* The object, whose representation may be better approached by photography, ceases to be the subject. There has been, in addition, the dissolution of the metaphysical grounding of objects from the combined perspectives of Kant and quantum physics.

ART AS PSYCHE'S CHILD

My first exposure to the psychological criticism of art came from the neo-Freudians, and I found their work to be reductionistic and in service to privileged ideologies. Much Jungian criticism has suffered from the same reductionism. Even when Jung himself ventured into the criticism of art, as in his essays on Joyce's *Ulysses* and Picasso, he might better have not written at all.

When asked the question "On what critical ground are we to stand?", I feel obliged to say that I value the partial truths of virtually every critical approach there is. However, when I reflect on why I have valued psychology but loved art, why I find the arts a more reliable guide to human history, behavior, and hidden motive than may be found in books of psychology, I am driven to confess a personal bias. I find myself treasuring that which stirs my imagination, moves me deeply, and opens me to enlarged vision, no matter how or in what fashion this may be done. When we are in the presence of art that does all these things, we find, in James Hillman's words, "There is no end to depth, and all things become soul."[1] I find myself treasuring that art which brings me into proximity with the gods. Here again, Hillman reminds us what is meant by that term *gods:* "In archetypal psychology gods are *imagined* . . . They are formulated ambiguously, as metaphors for modes of experience and as numinous borderline persons. They are cosmic perspectives in which the soul participates."[2]

So, what moves us is the encounter with the depths, with the godly, whether consciously processed or not. And what moves us most deeply is *something which we are also,* otherwise we remain indifferent to it. The principle of resonance is critical here, for resonance tells us what is true for us, or what moves us. Resonance is not created by an act of will; it is experienced autonomously, the stirring of "like to like," the thrum of the tuning fork inside of us. Such experience, as Plato noted long ago in his dialogue called *The Meno,* is always re-cognition, the re-membering of some lost wholeness as we encounter its numinous parts. This critical place to stand, that all art is psyche's child, is itself a metaphor, of course, but it acknowledges the power of the archetypal imagination to move us and to bring us into proximity with our source. Once again, Hillman: "Within the metaphorical perspective, within the imaginal field, nothing is more sure than the soul's own activity.... Thus the soul finds psyche everywhere, recognizes itself in all things, all things providing psychological reflection. And the soul accepts itself in the mythical enactments as one more such metaphor. More real than itself, more ultimate than its psychic metaphor, there is nothing."[3]

In sum, our critical place on which to stand depends itself on metaphor. To recall that all standpoints are metaphors is to be saved from literalism, from ideological idolatry, and from the fundamentalism of that psychosis which confuses objects with their names. The standpoint, then, is the metaphor of *soul* which allows us to be moved by the gods, those powers who are themselves metaphors. Retaining our ability to reflect on metaphor allows us to accept the autonomy of the mysteries and to remain open to their unpredictable visitations. So, all we can say in the presence of art which moves us is that we have been visited by the gods, with metaphor as the tangible trace of the encounter.

The Metarealism of Meaning

In speaking on several occasions to the Richmond, Virginia, Jungian society, I have had the privilege of staying in the home of Nancy Witt, one of the group's founders, in Ashland, Virginia. Nancy lives in a nineteenth-century mill, over a stream and a waterwheel, beside a pond, in some of the most historic land of our nation.

When I first visited Richmond and walked into that mill, I was stunned by the thirty-plus paintings that line the spacious walls of two floors and create not only a museum effect but also a sanctuary for meditation and reflection. Nancy has created a body of work over the last twenty-some years which incarnates a deeply religious and archetypal vision of eternity. Her favorite critical review came from an unlettered man who was helping unload her paintings for display at a conference in New Hampshire. This hotel worker went about and gathered other employees, and she overheard him say to them, "Come, you have to see these paintings. They are religious!" So, I say to you, come see these paintings; they are religious.

We are all familiar with the moment when painting discovered psychoanalysis and produced surrealism. I have always been drawn to the work of René Magritte and Salvador Dali. Although we may not profess to understand their work, the art speaks to that part of our souls whence our dreams emanate. Within the painter's frame, familiar objects are melted, dis-located, or distorted into affectively charged states. We will be just as comfortable or uncomfortable with their work as we are with our own dream life. The capacity of the ego to accept ambiguity is central to emotional maturity. In fact, how we can hold what I call the triple A's—ambiguity, ambivalence, and anxiety—in tension is a test of our psychic strength, which can even be reflected in our aesthetic tastes. Those who say, "I know what I like," are really saying, "I like what I know." Thus, the surrealists are celebrated because we all intuit that they are on to something, that they are reflecting something very deep within our time and our psyches, even as they are ridiculed, even reviled, as a means of keeping their visitations to the underworld at a safe distance.

Nancy Witt describes herself as a "metarealist," however. Perhaps the best way to understand this term is to think of Kafka, that compatriot of Rilke, who, with his strange parabolic stories, novels, and aphorisms, stood, according to Auden, in relationship to our troubled times as Dante stood as the chief visionary of his. When you think of Kafka's stories, they are eminently ratiocinative and realistic, once you accept an emotional premise. For example, in "Metamorphosis," once we accept that Gregor Samsa can be transformed into an insect, a metaphor for radical depersonalization, all else flows logically and sequentially. Or once we accept that we may be guilty without having done anything, that life is neither fair nor rational, then we may share Joseph K.'s search for clarity and justice with both sympathy and detachment.

Kafka, in my view, is a metarealist, for he takes ordinary events and turns them ever so slightly so that we are obliged to question what reality may be. Often we are left in the position of not knowing what the reality may be, for it has been called into profound question. The familiar lens through which we see the world has been turned a few degrees, and while the world remains recognizable, it is no longer familiar, safe, or predictable. While the impact of Kafka's vision was often disturbing, even chilling, it was in fact exceeded by the surrealism of European history in the twentieth century.

Nancy Witt's metarealism has to do with opening our eyes to see through the ordinary phenomenal world into the epiphanic world, that is, the world of revelatory vision. In this sense she is like Blake as well— one who said that while many saw only a ball of gold in the sky, he saw the Lord God Almighty and heard celestial choirs.

Metarealism is an expression of primordial experience which then runs through the aesthetic alembic of the artist and thereby is ordered. But it arises out of a place which may be disordered and chaotic, which bespeaks the wild precincts of nature. The rending of the curtain allows us to see that, behind the curtain, there is another world of appearances, and behind that another world as well. One who is drawn to do this work has no choice, actually, for as Jung writes, "for all the freedom of [the artist's] life and the clarity of his thought, he is everywhere hemmed around and prevailed upon by the Unconscious, the mysterious god within him, so that ideas flow to him—he knows not whence, he is driven to work and create—he knows not to what end, and is mastered by an impulse for constant growth and development— he knows not whither."[4]

Nancy labors in her studio every day but Sunday from at least 9:00 A.M. to 5:00 P.M. Why? Because she has to. She told me that she plans to work in this way until she dies because there is so little time and so many images are clamoring for her attention. She told me that very rarely has she begun a painting with an idea in mind. More often she has simply been drawn to an object and then she begins to see through the object to the worlds behind it. Or she has a certain "feeling state"/ and looks for images which will somehow incarnate that state.

I talked once with the late metarealistic painter Frank Howell, whose heritage was both Sioux and Anglo. He said that his best work seemed to come from those moments when some force within the canvas that wanted to come forth nudged aside his original idea. When he was able to let go of the ego's idea and give form and color to the emergent energy, he found those were the paintings which most spoke to other people. When I suggested that he was at those moments the vehicle of the archetypal imagination, he said that concept had no meaning to him. As Jung suggested, the artist is prevailed upon by the unconscious, and ideas flow to him or her from the Mysterious Other. He or she is a person driven by the gods to work, worry, and joy in the creative act.

The sculptor Henry Moore once observed of his decades of creativity that he had a passion so great that he could not chip it all away. When we recall that *passio* is Latin for "suffering," we understand the suffering which is implicit in all creativity. Moreover, the artist is mastered by his or her own need for personal growth, the growth which comes when we attend our individuation imperative. We are forever being surprised by what lies behind the next developmental door. And we are often obliged to go to places we would rather not, but to which some larger power insists we go.

So, Nancy paints every day, all day, producing a new large painting about once a month. She could be watching television, or shopping, but she chooses to be with her muse and to create.

OPENING: REALITY'S RENT CURTAIN

In this first painting, titled *Opening*, we see our definitions of reality opened as a curtain is opened. We see what appears conventional: a landscape with earth, and hills, and clouds. But in the newly opened center we glimpse the *Mare nostrum*, the sea as the primal symbol of the unconscious itself, trackless, unfathomable, and omnipresent. And

Figure 1. Opening. *1978. Oil on linen. 30" x 40".*

are those the artist's feet, her standpoint, at the bottom of the painting? Is the ground upon which we stand ever firm, fixed, and reliable? And whose hands pull aside the fabric of reality? We are often moved by such invisible powers whether we know it or not. Rilke mused on how lovers are moved by deep forces not their own: "Upon what instrument have we been strung? / And in the hands of what musician are we held?"[5]

Of this painting Nancy wrote, "when I don't have a clear idea of what wants to be painted, I will frequently paint a sky that appeals to me over water. Usually right at the shoreline, at the edge—where water and land meet—I find that if I watch there long enough something will appear. It's where consciousness and the unconscious meet."[6]

This description of the creative process might be called a form of active imagination. This technique so common to Jungian parlance is still often misunderstood. Jung did not mean free association, meditation, or guided imagery. Active imagination needs to be understood literally as the *activation of the image,* a technique which invites *Auseinandersetzung* or a dialogue with the unconscious. Active imagination affords the unconscious its own freedom, its own integrity. It seeks an expanded consciousness, which arises out of an encounter with the intrapsychic Other.

Nancy is describing the encounter with the Other which arises out of her capacity to relinquish ego control and to allow herself to be open to the mystery. When the objects themselves begin to speak, when they begin to unfold themselves, then we are in proper relationship to nature, for we are respectfully allowing it its autonomy of being. Such an attitude is essentially religious in character for it relocates the ego in the presence of the transcendent Other. The experience of the mystery of the Other is phenomenological, and our subsequent consciousness of it is epiphenomenological; that is to say, primordial experience may lead to the secondary and attendant experience of consciousness. Nancy also writes that the "thing" excites libido and she is invited to a dynamic dialogue with it: "Eventually a dialogue develops between me and the image, which grows and changes in response to what's inside my head."[7]

We see here that consciousness is not abandoned; it is enlarged and still plays a role in the individuation process. Another way of saying this is that fate, or the gods, determined that Nancy's work of individuation would arise out of her dialogue with things and out of the autonomy of images which derive from that dialogue. For other individuals the dialogue will arise from dream work, or the complexities of relationship, or by following their daimon, wheresoever it wishes to take them.

The quotidian questions we may have about *Opening* will not be answered. What does it mean? Whose feet are those? Whose hands pull back the fabric? Are the male hands allusions to specific figures or animus attitudes, in which case the painting is more allegorical than symbolic? All we can safely say is that the painting calls our conventional sense of reality into question. When this relocation of reality occurs, we are in the presence of the visionary. Similarly, the holographic Blake said one could see eternity in a grain of sand.

The viewer stands on the edge of the known world and stares off into eternity. As we know, Archimedes once said that if he had a place to stand he could move the world. For the last four centuries the common ground upon which the Western world once stood has been eroding. Necessarily, the task of meaning ineluctably shifted from tribal mythologies, institutional formulations, and conventional pieties to the shoulders of the individual. As the mythic power of church and monarchy have waned, so the points of reference have disappeared. The spiritual anarchy which follows is aided in part by the capacity of the artist to nominate a point of reference, and from that point recreate the world. While *Opening* suggests that the world is far more mysterious than we might have thought, it also presents us with a fascinating aperture which takes us into a deeper plane. As we contemplate that mystery, we sense that something may be contemplating us. As we watch, perhaps we are being watched as well.

INSIDE: THE OBJECTIFICATION OF SUBJECTIVITY

In the painting *Inside* we see Nancy at her work desk in apparent contemplation and an image of a triangle within a circle. While the artist's tools are present and the canvas waits, there is no mood for stroke or figure yet. On the left of the canvas we see a hanging lightbulb, something of a cultural convention for an illumination, but we surmise that

that bulb will end up much more integrated into the final painting, which is yet to be done. And yet we are looking at the finished painting already, are we not?

The triangular shapes, both on the canvas within the canvas and the lighting above the painter, are themselves archetypal, three being the number of creative power, of dynamism. But these triangles are also contained by circles, mandalic rounds which imply closure and completion. One remembers the famous alchemical formula of Maria Prophetissa from the Middle Ages, namely: out of the one comes the two, and out of the two comes the three, and out of the three comes the four which shall become one. What the formulary suggests is that out of the one of undifferentiated unconsciousness will come the two which beget both consciousness and the splitting of neurosis. Out of that split the reconciling third, which contains the opposites, will emerge and dynamically spill over into the four, which is the tension of opposites evolved to a higher level. Out of this more evolved tension of opposites, the possibility of the new One may emerge.

This portrait of a portrait, this painter painting herself, is itself a part of the *trompe l'oeil* of reflectivity. We reflect upon ourselves reflecting upon ourselves. In this moment the subject seems transfixed by a process. She appears captured by the power of the triangle, the tetragram, the mandala, and something profound is moving in her. And yet Nancy the painter has painted herself in this position, suggesting not only the awareness of that moment of transfixion, but of having also moved through it to something else. How many great poems came from the Romantic poets, from "Kubla Khan" to "Ode on Dejection," in which the poet writes movingly about creative blockage, writes creatively about the loss of creativity? Here the painter paints herself, not painting, but being moved toward painting. Is it a painting almost about painting, then, or is not every painting since the impressionists about painting itself?

Moreover, we see that the boundary of the painting within the painting has been framed by the painter. The space in which her subject contemplates is itself encapsulated as it exists in a realm unto itself, which perhaps it does. What then constitutes the empty spaces to the right and left of the capsule? Do they not exist to remind us of the ar-

Figure 2. Inside. *1973. Oil on canvas with construction. 42" x 60".*

bitrary point of view of this artist, that she has created her own place of reference and that it lies not within the confines of the painting but within the confines of her psyche, a reality which greatly transcends the conscious frame of reference?

And lastly, the title of the painting, *Inside*—inside of what? Are we inside the studio, inside the mind of the subject of the painter, inside the mind of the painter herself? Are we inside always because, as Kant insisted, the world itself is unknowable, and we can only provisionally know what we have experienced inwardly? Kant demolished metaphysics by removing the Archimedean point of the philosopher, thus making psychology necessary. Psychology's most difficult task then becomes to reflect upon itself, to not be the disease of what it is meant to cure, as Wittgenstein once said of philosophy. *Inside* reminds us that we are always inside, that such is our condition, although the world out there beckons, visits, eludes, and confounds.

CAPRON: THE PRESENCE OF THOSE ABSENT

At Nancy's mill, the room in which I stay has the painting entitled *Capron* on the wall. At first glance I thought I saw Freud in the background. Upon close inspection I realized that it was a stranger. I learned later that the image of the couple standing there is taken from a photo of Nancy's paternal grandparents. The snapshot pinned to the easel is a photo of her father, and the setting is the house in which they lived in the village of Capron, Virginia. Of these figures, Nancy told me, "Both men were Methodist preachers. Near the end of his life I went with my Father to visit that area in Southeast Virginia and that house. While I was making the painting I noticed that the fireplace was bricked up. About that time I learned from an aunt that my Grandfather 'burned out' long before retirement age. It seemed to me that my Father experienced something similar not long before his death. So it seemed important that I note that the fire had shifted from some 'place' elsewhere."[8]

In the picture the couple seem attired in clothing which vaguely indicates a time and a class, and their attitude seemingly reflects a degree of confidence or at the least nonchalant familiarity with who they are, perhaps only because of a strong sense of role identity. In front is a chalice, which reappears in several of Nancy's works. While the im-

Figure 3. Capron. *1989. Oil on linen. 30" x 36".*

ages of the painting are heretofore both conventional and highly personal, we sense that the chalice has a significance which extends beyond the mere representation of a historical image. At this point, as in the task of dream interpretation, we necessarily differentiate the role of personal image, which may more properly be called *sign*, and that of symbol. The depiction of the bricked-up fireplace, for example, is an allegorical use of image in a one-to-one level of reference. "Blocked fire," so to speak, equals "blocked 'fire.'"

Obviously, the implicit reference to blocked fire moves us toward the allegorical and symbolic when we consider what blockage is and what fire is. Even without Nancy's identification of the allegorical use of the fireplace image, we might stumble toward a notion of why the artist might have employed such an image. We might conclude that the fires of certain energies are no longer regnant or available. However, with the image of the chalice we intuit that we are more properly in that zone of ambiguity we call the symbolic. Generally speaking, the chalice, whether it be the lost grail of medieval legend or the chalice crushed beneath the bridegroom's heel, is a vessel which contains the sacred. That this chalice holds a flickering flame suggests to us an homage, or at least respect for, the continued power of the ancestral even as we might find in a Japanese Shinto temple.

What Nancy Witt is attempting in *Capron* illustrates the veracity of T. S. Eliot's observation about history, that it is not the pastness of the past which is important, but the continuing *presence* of the past. As therapists will testify, few powers are mightier than those which we call the parental complexes, which operate more autonomously within us because we are not conscious of them. They are present in our choices and in our sense of self, and for good or ill they color our intimate relationships. This insight, which is illustrated in genograms (used by therapists to outline familial patterns of behavior) and case histories and in the resonant reservoirs of dream imagery, is hardly new.

Greek mythology and tragedy sought to account for the replication of familial patterns, for the power of invisible cause and effect, and for the occasional madness which usurped reason and common sense. How could Oedipus be the carrier of the sins of the House of Thebes, or Electra and Orestes the unwitting bearers of generations of the House of Atreus? They concluded that some historic offense to the gods had occasioned a blood curse, which rippled through the generations until suffering and penance produced sufficient consciousness to achieve right relationship before the gods again. History is not only the story of the individual writ large, as Emerson and Carlyle suggested, but the exfoliation and extrapolation of those intrapsychic imagoes which Jung called "complexes" and which are transmitted, not only through outer example and admonition, but also invisibly through the unconscious.

Let me illustrate in a quite personal way. One summer I was invited to speak in Stockholm and Solna, Sweden. While my ancestry was Swedish (my long-deceased grandfather was named Gustav Lindgren, and he had arrived in the New World in 1900), there was never any talk about Sweden in our household. Even my mother had not spoken of her father, whom she never really knew because he had died in a coal-mining accident when she was quite young. On my first night in Sweden, we went to an outdoor restaurant for dinner. At dusk, the audience rose and sang the national anthem as the flag was lowered. At that moment a powerful voice echoed in my head, saying, "I have come back for you."

I was stunned by this voice and knew its meaning immediately, namely, that I, the third generation, had returned home for those who had been unable to and who had, like most Americans, never consciously considered the idea. (While studying in Switzerland, I learned that Europeans consider the influence of nation much more seriously than we of the New World who not only melted into the national pot but also believe that we have invented ourselves by overthrowing the presumed tyranny of the past.) Moreover, while traveling through southern Sweden, whence the Lindgrens would have come, I had numerous experiences which could only be described as *déjà vu*. I was further told by many Swedes that I looked, acted, and spoke like a Swede though I spoke only in English. All this was and would remain puzzling and irrational to me were it not for one possibility, namely, the transmission of the parental heritage through the unconscious.

The more we know about our biologies, the more we learn of our genetic coding; the more we learn of depth psychology, the more we discern the movement of the silent generations within us. In eliciting the parent's parents, Nancy Witt is intuitively evoking the multiple generations which are at work within her own contemporary psychological reality. Freud once observed that when a couple goes to bed, at least four others are present, namely, the parents as complexes. We know that at least the parents' parental complexes influenced our notions of self, relationship, sexuality, and the like, so already there are at least fourteen in bed, and all are active.

Jung took the power of such spectral presences very seriously. In an essay written in 1919 and titled, "The Psychological Foundation for the Belief in Spirits," he noted that we find in all traditions "a universal belief in the existence of phantoms or ethereal beings who dwell in the neighbourhood of men and who exercise an invisible yet powerful influence upon them. These beings are generally supposed to be spirits or souls of the dead."[9] Our predecessors knew what depth psychology has had to rediscover for us: that we live simultaneously in two worlds, the world of the senses and the invisible world which is haunted by spectral presences which we call *complexes,* or *projections.* Jung reminds us of the power of these presences in his statement that "many patients feel persecuted by their parents long after they are dead."[10] The word which Jung used to describe our experience of these phenomena was *Ergriffenheit,* which one may translate as the ego's experience of being seized or possessed by the power of an other.

Just as the ancients dramatized this possessive power in the tales of wronged gods, hybristic patriarchs, and humbled grandchildren, so we seek a different language for the same phenomena. Thus Jung writes, "Spirits . . . viewed from the psychological angle, are unconscious autonomous complexes which appear as projections because they have no direct association with the ego."[11] When our ancestors experienced such possession by spectral presences, they employed the metaphor of the loss of soul. We use a more impoverished language and speak of neurosis. Our ancestors recognized two forms of spiritual malady: the loss of soul and possession by malignant spirits. We more vaguely talk of not feeling ourselves, for some complex has robbed our energy, or of being in the grip of a pervasive mood for unaccountable reasons. Our presumed gain through such clinical imagery is at the expense of the imaginal which moves the heart. An affectively charged image, such as spirit possession, will always touch us more deeply than an enervated, clinical language which pretends to accuracy but which deanimates nature and denudes the gods.

We have all experienced this form of possession, or this loss of soul. It feels uncanny, frightening, alienating, humbling. Even nations can collectively experience the loss of soul, as they are separated from their psychic roots, or spirit possession, when consciousness is enervated and they are at the mercy of fads, fashions, or malignant spirits. However, the reintegration of such energies, whether through the traditional powers of the shamans, tribal mythologies, the work of psychoanalysis, or the inexplicable grace of consciousness, makes the split-off energies available to ego once more and one feels a sense of well-being.

What Nancy is doing in this painting is to consciously evoke the parent's parents (for she senses they are present beyond the limits of death, memory, and conscious influence) and to light a candle of consciousness in the great darkness, which Jung has described as our fundamental task. We know that divorce does not end a marriage, nor death end the influence of a parent, nor time erase the power of primal epiphanies. Jung describes the mechanism by which this continuing power occurs: "When a person dies, the feelings and emotions that bound his relatives to him lose their application to reality and sink into the unconscious, where they activate a collective content that has a deleterious effect on consciousness."[12]

Perhaps what the gods demand of us is not slavish worship, nor infantilizing imitation, or apotropaic denial, but simply to be remembered, to be respected as the truths which do not die as everything else will. To hold a candle of consciousness in the darkness, to pay homage to the power of the multigenerational influences which we carry into daily life, means that our relationships with the past might prove less troubled and our movement through the twin worlds which we inhabit might be richer.

SUE'S FAN: THE METONYMIES OF MEMORY

After my maternal grandmother died, I wrote a poem of praise for her. It is impossible of course to summon up the whole experience of a person. So rich and variegated is our experience that we may render only a small part of it conscious. Of the many images which flooded

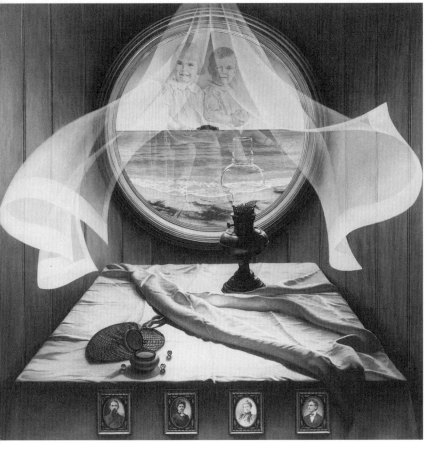

Figure 4. Sue's Fan. *1988. Oil on linen. 48" x 48".*

me, one in particular took me back to the wonder of childhood. My grandmother worked a great deal in roses, and her wrists were often scratched from this occupation. As a child, full of wonder and terror, I observed much and pondered even more. These scratches both frightened me and fascinated me, and bound me to her through her work with flowers. The concluding lines of the poem, then, were redolent of these images:

> . . . *roses and thorn-bitten wrists,*
> *blood, and first blood,*
> *in the first scratch of time.*

The initial reference to blood is of the bloody scratches, and the second refers to me, her first grandchild. But the scratch suggests that these wounds are only the first of many to follow, not the least of which being mortality itself, not only for the deceased grandmother but also for the child who will follow in her ash-bound steps. The focus on the scratches is the metonymy of memory, a means by which that which is associated may be utilized to summon up the whole. We can never summon the whole, but if we are wise or lucky we will find the key association which may evoke the power of the whole.

Anyone who works with dreams will testify to this common power of the dream-maker to find such images which suggest, which intimate, which conjure up the larger powers. Moreover, the blood scratch is itself symbolic of the mystery of incarnation, of the relationships of generations through the bloodline, and of the mortality which we carry in our sanguinary sojourns.

In the painting *Sue's Fan,* Nancy has similarly focused on a memory of her grandmother. The particular fan reminds us of the era before air-conditioning, when every home and church and workplace had such fans as necessary instruments of survival. We also observe a vessel of some unguent for the skin, earrings, and a lamp which is no longer lit. Each of these images is a thesaurus for the painter and tied to her specific experience, yet each has the power to summon us to memory and to the power of metonymy.

Of the figures represented, Nancy wrote, "the figures in *Sue's Fan* are both sets of grandparents—more different from each other than you could imagine. I was named for both grandmothers—Nancy Sue. Very Southern. Nancy taught me: 'When e'er a task awaits you, with solemn judgment view it; don't sit and idly wish it done, begin at once and do it.' [On the other hand] Sue: 'Whether a task be great or small, do it well or not at all,' which somehow got translated into 'Don't bother.'"[13]

The way in which the portraits of the four grandparents are arranged reminds one of a portion of a genogram. From such primal sources come strong genes along with their moralizing rhymes and admonitions. While Nancy the painter wryly suggests that no small part of her life may have been lived in rebellion against those constricting expectations, she acknowledges that she is of her grandmothers' blood in more than her amalgamated name. Perhaps the woman who dares to stand for forty and fifty hours a week before her canvas is doing exactly what those maxims intended. "With solemn judgment view it . . . begin and do it . . . task do well or not at all. . . . " How many of us have spent our lives rebelling against admonitions and expectations and running in the opposite direction only to find that we have fulfilled the expectations in some cleverly disguised manner?

The children who spectrally sit in the window are Nancy and her brother, the issue and descendants of these primal sources. We sense that they surely were implicit in the beginnings, for we are all born before we are born, in our parents' dreams and in their genetic coding. We sense that they too are evanescent, as flimsy as that blowing curtain. We sense in the lantern without light some missing insight, some enlightening perspective. In the distance lies the happy isle, some valorized Valhalla that one glimpses and never fully attains. It is always out there, in sight, just now slipping over the horizon. Surely these images, particular to a Virginia painter, are images which depict our condition as well.

And of all the things upon which to focus, and to name the painting, why Sue's fan? Why not Nancy's earrings? Why not a curtain in the wind? The particularity of the fan intrigues. As a specific artifact of memory it is as tied to her ancestral source as my grandmother's rose-bitten wrists. Yet such artifacts of memory stir the inexpressible world of childhood with its plethora of affectively charged images. Rilke wrote of his childhood, and out of the vast phantasmagoria of memory he settled on the ball with which they played. He celebrated its luscious, tactile curve, and yet, alas, how those mortal children stepped under the falling ball. In one image—the ball—Rilke conjures both the innocent game of childhood and the perilous perigee of their curving descent toward death.

Sue's fan is shaped like a heart; it points away from the children, yet its stem is bound to them, and it lies under a shroud unveiled for the moment, in an instance as fleeting as the whip and flash of a gauzy curtain in the wind. In such moments, flooded by the permutating powers of the past, fleeting memory binds the far-flung islands of identity and knits psyche's cloth. Thus, for moments only, the curtains which tumble are like ghosts which remind.

CHALICE: THE GREAT MOTHER'S CHILD

Many of Nancy's paintings feature this same chalice, which is based on a rather ordinary-looking metal cup in her cupboard. But that cup becomes transformed in her paintings as we have seen, and in *Chalice* it is central to her vision.

And what is the chalice which haunts and holds so many of our projections? As we know, the grail imago has functioned within the Christian tradition as the cup which held the wine become blood of Christ which, though lost, still carries the projection of the search for divinity. Another tradition has it that the chalice was fashioned from an emerald dropped from Lucifer's forehead when he fell headlong into the abyss. The archetypal imagination further employs the chalice as the container, that which receives, holds, and perhaps alchemically transforms. In this particular painting the chalice seems overflowing with the effluvia of the great sea behind it, a primal symbol of the *Magna Mater,* the nurturant matrix from which all things come. Sand, sea, rocky shoal, and sky all meet here; the four-fold venues of the world gather at the point of the sacred container. What does knit our lives, our histories, our memories? What keeps constancy, if not the containing vessel which we call soul? The pre-Socratic Heraclitus averred that the human soul was a distant land whose boundaries could never be found. Only through such images as the chalice can we have a bridge to the invisible world, without which we live in emptiness.

WINDOWS: THROUGH A GLASS DARKLY

Our lives are suffused with stimuli of unimaginable proportion and unassimilable magnitude. One of the several functions of dreams seems to be to process the dross and detritus of daily life, to help us clear a space for the coming day. Inevitably, the influx of stimuli is dissociated

Figure 5. Chalice. *1988. Oil on linen. 40" x 52".*

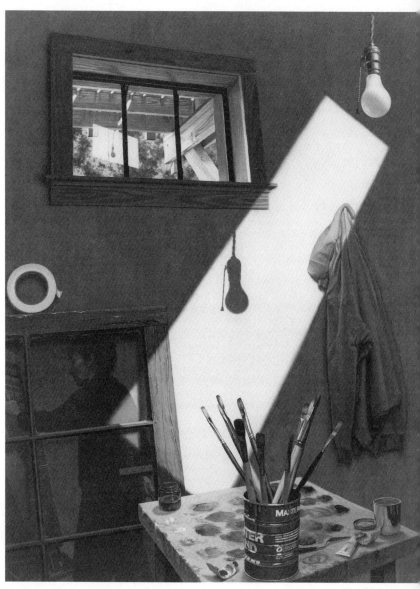

Figure 6. Windows. *1990. Oil on linen. 34" x 44".*

and rendered banal if observed at all. One of the gifts of the artist is to call attention to, to bring into focus, to lift the extraordinary out of the everyday. I have the privilege of living with an artist, and her way of seeing, her sensitivity to nuance of shade, texture, and form has obligated the expansion of my visual world. If Wordsworth could see in a moment's epiphany that the violet by the mossy stone was the work of eternity, then the gift of the artist is to make us mindful of those depths which course beneath all surfaces. As Éluard reminds, "There is another world, and it is this one."

In *Windows* we find an apparently banal scene, a basement, a workplace, a window which leads nowhere. But there is that lightbulb there again, as central as the light in *Guernica*. Yet it, too, has its shadow on the wall and reality is doubled. We have a mirror to the outside which does not reveal very much, and we have a glass frame against the wall, leading nowhere, which shows us the painter herself. Through the glass darkly (which, in the King James version of I Corinthians 13, meant to see oneself dimly in the mirror), one finds oneself now in a vertiginous world of planes and altered states. If that is the painter in the framed glass, then who is painting the painter, or from what perspective then are we seeing, or being seen? And what kind of window might it be which casts such rectangular light across the wall at such an angle unless the window itself is the begetter of our illumination, so that planes of reality cut across each other all the time? So we have glass through which we see, and glass in which we see ourselves; we have windows upon the banal and windows upon eternity; we have the painter painting a painting about a painter painting a painting, which is really about another subject, which is not clear, unless that which we thought clear and is not, is in fact the subject, and that these planes of reality intersect in our lives all the time, and that is the plain plane truth.

At the bottom in the center stands the homely can with the tools of the trade, and the brushes point in all the directions of the painting, even as the hands in *Guernica* reach for the light. And that light on the right is balanced by the obscure white circle of tape on the left. Is it a mandalic image, a casual object, or the empty eye of eternity?

This painting illustrates Jung's previously cited remarks about how primordial experience allows a glimpse into the abyss. We who seek may also be sought. It is well known that the inscription over the entrance to the temple of Apollo at Delphi offered the very sage advice, "Know Thyself." But it has been reported that over the entrance to the inner temple, which could be obtained only after a rigorous spiritual apprenticeship, there was inscribed, "Thou Art." We recall that *numinous* comes from a word meaning "to nod," and we need to remember that soul is found in all the world and autonomously seeks us as well. It nods at us as it solicits connection. This painting is the obverse of *Opening,* which typifies our search for the divine and suggests that the divine may well be searching for us.

Just as we frequently find strangers in our dreams who seem to know us, so there is something which is familiar in all of us, for we are of this contiguous cosmos—plant, animal, and soul, and only ego splits us off. We recall Hölderlin in "Patmos": "That which thou seekest is near, and / already coming to meet thee." Or Pascal's *pensée,* "Console thyself, thou woulds't not be seeking me hadst thou not already found me." Or Plato in the *Meno* that all knowledge is re-cognition of that which is primordially known.

What stands on the other side of that curtain, the limit of consciousness, the veil of mortality, the poverty of imagination? What reaches through toward us? What rends the quotidian plane of sea and surf and sky? And what do we see when we see through the glass darkly, or glimpse the other side for a moment? We see here, at least, a blank screen on which eternity, or the mind's eye, or our projections find their expression. What can we know of that other side? We can only be capable of that which we may know in this limited state, but there, beyond time and number, and space and limit, is our home, and we carry that same home within each of us. We resonate to such images because they are the carriers of such energy as courses through us even as it animates the cosmos. We are moved only by like to like. What beckons from the other side, and to whose mythic motions all of us move, is, in ways we could never comprehend, like us, of us, about us. Such an image as the

Figure 7. Second Opening. *1989. Oil on linen. 24" x 30".*

Second Opening is a window not only on eternity but on the infinite reaches of the human psyche as well.

Of *Rhyton* Nancy Witt said, "Rhyton is a Greek drinking cup. . . . I happen to own the one in the painting of that name—has to do with Bacchus in my mind, hence passion, fire, and all that good stuff."[14] In the effort to "image up," which is the contribution the archetypal imagination makes in our effort to approach the ineffable, we are present to something heating up. Of the twenty volumes of the *Collected Works*, Jung devoted three of them to alchemy. His interest in alchemy is enough to mark him suspect in most psychological circles, but he recognized that the alchemists were the last in the Western tradition to seek to hold spirit and matter together before their fatal fracturing into physics, chemistry, psychology, philosophy, medicine, and theology. Moreover, Jung recognized that there is no artifact of human culture which does not carry the imprint of the human psyche. Every psychology, he said, is a subjective confession, telling us more of the author than of the psyche. So, too, is every theology, for the mystery remains mysterious and ineffable.

Tracking the way in which the psyche structures this invisible world, as it does in our dreams each night or in our tribal mythologies, is a work requiring great patience but offering great reward. In *Rhyton*, the flammable materials of the psyche are stirring in the drinking cup. In that cup is the fruit of the vine, sacred to the dying god Dionysus-Bacchus, or later the blood of Christ. The transubstantiation of matter is the life-long goal of many religions, the transmutation of dross material into pure spirit. What breaks forth from this wine is the triple taurean imago of the bull, which is also associated with the *Magna Mater*. The sacrifice of the child to the Great Mother survives in the ritualized slaying of the bull in Spanish culture. The mythology of the dying-reborn god is central to the religions of the Near East, the stories of Adonis, Tammuz, Dionysus, Jesus Christ, and others, and partakes of that mythological movement we may call "the cycle of sacrifice." Two great mythic paradigms move the world: the linear, solar hero quest

Figure 8. Rhyton. *1986. Oil on linen. 46" x 46".*

which is developmental, and the lunar, cyclic birth-rebirth which dramatizes how life renews itself.

Both of these mythic paradigms may be found in some fashion in all cultures, for both are required to answer our questions as to how life moves forward and how life dies and is reborn. These patterns antedate Christianity by millennia, but, because they are archetypal, they illustrate how these primordial images are necessary to animate, to "image forth" later primordial experiences. Nancy may or may not consciously be drawing on these traditions, but that matters little, for these images have a life of their own. As Jung said, the archetypal images are formative patterns, which attract such materials as are useful for their representation or incarnation. From such heating up, the psyche fashions forth the transformation of wine into spirit and of those who drink into divinity.

GLASS DARKLY: FOR NOW WE SEE CLEARLY

What, we may ask, is the subject of this painting, *Glass Darkly?* Is it the objects on the canvas? Is it the painter herself? Is it the painter painting? Is it meant to induce questioning about the separate but intersecting planes of reality? Since the invention of the daguerreotype in the 1830s, painting has been released from any obligation to reproduce a photographic version of reality. Perhaps the best contribution of any art is to provide an angle of vision, as long as we recall that the painting is to oblige our questioning of the variegated versions of ontic reality.

In establishing the wine bottle and fruit, the painter invokes the painterly interest in surfaces and planes, vertical, angular, and spheroid. In showing herself painting these objects she suggests her lineage from at least Cézanne to the present. In positioning the worker's glove and a used tube of acrylic she reminds us that what she does is her work, a labor from nine to five, six days a week. And yet by tearing the horizontal strip across the canvas, a *trompe l'oeil,* which is not a tear at all, she reminds us of the planes within planes which exist simultaneously. Only consciousness intersects these planes.

In a poem titled "A High-toned Old Christian Woman," Wallace Stevens asserts that he, the poet, and she, the theologue, are about the same process, the making of fictions. But the poet remains metaphysically and psychologically free in his awareness of the fictive nature of all knowledge and the provisionality of all perspectives, while she remains trapped in her idolatrous literalism. Such fictions are necessary, coming from *facere* in Latin, meaning "to make," for all constructs are things made. To fall in love with our own constructs and believe that they contain the mystery is blasphemous, for such reification seeks to colonize the mystery on behalf of ego's dominion. This modern sensibility is required since depth psychology has taught us that each state-

(88)   ARCHETYPAL IMAGINATION

Figure 9. Glass Darkly. *1982. Oil on linen. 36" x 42".*

ment about reality is an implicit Rorschach of our own mind. What Blake called "reorganized innocence" is necessary to spare us from the sin of literalism, which is an unintended insult to the autonomy and complexity of mystery. As Stevens concludes his poem, "This will make widows wince. But fictive things / Wink as they will. Wink most when widows wince."[15] The wink is not only the numinous winking at us, but we need to wink back to be conscious of the game of fictions which we employ to approach the holy. Nancy Witt's planes upon planes, painted by the painter painting herself, is a supreme act of consciousness of the ineffable, of the wonderful tool that art may be for us when we approach the numinous, and of the need to wink as a measure of respect for the mystery.

In *Painting* Nancy tells us what we are observing: a painting, with the now familiar elements of surf, sea, and sky, stretching out to the horizon of the imaginal. Having lived only a mile from the Atlantic Ocean for nearly twenty years, I know how clichéd the portraits of the sea are—depictions of romantically tossed surf, nostalgic blankets and umbrellas for tourists to take back to the heartland. But that is not what we encounter in *Painting.* As before, *Painting* is about a painting which is about painting. And what is the act of painting about? Is it a recollection of the eye and memory? A photograph captures that moment, but a moment is evanescence itself, and so the painting seeks to capture an essence which extends beyond the transient to the essential.

Ostensibly this painting is of a seascape in which the demarcation between object and replication disappears as the margin of the canvas within the canvas merges with the background of the painting and becomes one. Yet the painting at the center of *Painting* depicts the triangular opening in the clouds even as the wave lines coincide exactly, suggesting again the mixing of planes of reality. In addition, we ask where the painter is, the painter who sat in that barber's seat. Why there she is, silhouetted on the sand before her easel, but it cannot be this easel, so that shadowy figure must be painting a painting other than this one. And who, we ask, is painting a painting titled *Painting* in which there is a painting alongside of which is a silhouette of a painter painting another painting while all of this has presumably been painted by still another painter? Who is the painter of these painters, then? We may answer that question only by knowing what we mean by God, who watches the universe, or the archetypal imagination which exists at multiple levels simultaneously. The only way in which we might be able to conjure with these multilayered intimations of reality is to accept the fictive character of what we hastily name reality and to realize that it is through the conscious use of the fictive (*facere,* "to make") that we become what Hermann Hesse called the *Magister Ludi der Glasperlin,* the masters of the glass bead game of the world. Only those who play the reality game consciously, that is, with the conscious use of image, metaphor, and symbol, are spared the self-deception of literalism.

Figure 10. Painting (V). *1984. Oil on linen. 38" diameter.*

BAILEY WON: REFRACTIONS OF TIME, PLACE, AND PERSON
Bailey Island, off the coast of Maine, is a place where Nancy often vacations in the summer, a place Jung himself visited, as did many of the first generation of analysts who studied under him. In the published collection of her paintings, Nancy writes, "In the summer of 1984 I spent several weeks on an island in Maine. I lived in a little red house perched on rocks with the wild Atlantic for my front yard. I had never lived alone before and experienced both freedom and hitherto unknown fears. . . .

There is a poem by Emily Dickinson in which she speaks of dwelling in possibility. My red house has come to be just such a dwelling for me."[16]

In the silhouette of the painter one senses the aloneness, the contemplative character of the moment and the work of the canvas within the canvas yet to be completed. As there is a canvas to fill, so there is a life to continue, to fill in new areas. In the homey V-8 can at the right we find the tools, the brushes, and the oils, and from the shadowed recesses of the artist we know the images will arise to reflect not only the wild Atlantic but the imaginative sensibility which brings order and meaning and, as Rilke noted in the *Duino Elegies,* which summons up being itself through the evocations of consciousness. In this painting we not only see again the multiple levels of reality, with even an awaiting easel in the Atlantic itself, but the true subject—found in the act of consciousness which makes meaning possible.

In the center is a bowl of water which intimates that smaller source we carry within us, the personal unconscious, which is itself a portion of the oceanic background of the collective unconscious. Through these two alembics, bowl and sea, personal and collective unconscious, the same energy flows. Things above are copies of things below; the human psyche is the receptacle of the oceanic energies and, in turn, brings the incarnational power of the particular. Without the cosmic energies, the individual would not live; without the individual, the cosmos would never be incarnated. It is only the limits of our ego-consciousness which object to the flowing of one reality, one canvas over into another, when in the imaginal world all is one. The archetypal Fall from undifferentiated bliss into consciousness created number, twoness, and only the archetypal imagination has the power to recover the unity which courses through this universe of "the ten thousand things."

From this title, *Bailey Won,* we sense that not only has the painter had to wrest from loneliness and disorientation a new sense of identity but a mythological grounding as well. The woman who can go through this time of loss of others, and points of reference, is obliged to discover that the longitudes and latitudes of the soul are within. She has learned that the silence is not silent, and that the dark is luminous. She has, in her loneliness, achieved solitude. When one is not alone when one is alone, when one is aware of a goodly presence within one-

Figure 11. Bailey Won. *1985. Oil on linen. 30" x 36".*

self, then one has achieved solitude. Our popular culture is a tacit agreement to flee the terror of loneliness, and it therefore circumvents the possibility of solitude. The avoidance of solitude is the flight, ultimately, from oneself. Paradoxically, it is only in solitude that our creativity and our gift to others will be found. As Jung has written so provocatively, "Individuation cuts one off from personal conformity and hence from collectivity. That is the guilt which the individual leaves behind . . . for the world, that is the guilt he must endeavor to redeem. He must offer a ransom in place of himself, that is, he must bring forth values which are an equivalent substitute for his absence in the collective personal sphere."[17]

The suffering of loneliness brings the encounter with the Self, which is found in the attainment of solitude, which becomes the source from which the new, the unique images of the individual arise to enhance, differentiate, and expand the collective sphere. The meaning of suffering is to find what that suffering may mean, and out of this discovery the person grows, contributes new values to the collective, and thereby wins the battle of Bailey Island.

CICATRICE: HEALING THE WORLD3S WOUND

In *Cicatrice,* an archaic word meaning scar, we recall the earlier images of *Opening* and *Second Opening.* The former summoned us to look below the visible world and see the vertiginous depths, and the latter alerted us to the autonomy of the numinous which winks, intimates, and invites rapprochement. Here we see no painter's silhouette, no canvas upon canvas, but the familiar elements of surf, sea, and sky are again transmogrified. The rent fabric is knit together, somewhat humorously by the incongruity of adhesive bandages, as if to make it impossible for us not to remember we are seeing a painting, but that the painting is as valuable a point of entry into the mystery of ordinary life as any metaphysics, any science, any theology.

It is precisely at the point of the split where the numinous and the opening of consciousness to depth touch. Such a contact, and such an *Auseinandersetzung,* to use one of Jung's favorite words, constitutes the activity of what he called the transcendent function. While we cannot know that other world, be it the cosmos without or the cosmos within,

Figure 12. Cicatrice. *1994. Oil on linen. 23" x 32".*

we may receive intimations from attendance upon their meeting point in vestigial images. We do not know, for example, the unconscious, but we have a dream image which presents itself to waking consciousness. Such an image bridges two worlds and partakes of both. The assimilation of such images into consciousness enlarges and nourishes conscious life. Without such access to depth we remain superficial and without vitality.

Yet the paradox of consciousness, for all its gifts, is found in the splitting upon which it is based. Without the splitting of the primal unity, consciousness cannot be birthed, but such splitting splinters and separates. Our ancestors dramatized this sundering separation as the Fall. The bandages remind us that such wounds are never wholly healed. They constitute the condition of mortal beings who have visions of divinity, who, though mortal, write immortal symphonies and poems, and paint openings to eternity. *Cicatrice* is the world's wound, never wholly healed, taped together, and yet the meeting point from which consciousness and creativity are found. As Odysseus was recognized by the faithful servant Euraclea by his wound, as Shakespeare's Coriolanus displayed his wounds as signature of his service to Rome, as Jesus was recognized by his astonished disciples on the road to Emmaus, so we are the carriers of the cicatrice which is our condition, our wound, and our unfolding splendor.

RING OF FIRE: CREATIVE CONFLAGRATION

As a last sample of the personal and archetypal imagination at work, we see *Ring of Fire*. At the center is the same rent between this world and the other, between the *Sehnsucht für Ewigekeit* and the summons of the nodding numinous, between the world's wound and the transcendent function's linkage. This time a flower breaks forth. From our deepest wound incredible beauty may be born. The Jesuit poet Gerard Manley Hopkins speaks of the transformative mystery, of how humans are born of the sod, of how from matter springs the mystery of soul, of how from the crimson defeat on the cross springs the alchemical gold: "blue-bleak embers . . . fall, gall themselves, and gash gold-vermillion."[18] The familiar sand, surf, and sky are now muted yet transfigured by the same image Dante used to represent the beatific vision—the multifoliate rose.

Figure 13. Ring of Fire. *1992. Oil on linen. 52" x 52".*

Of this painting Nancy wrote, "In meditation this morning I heard 'Be still my soul' and for the first time wondered why on Earth anyone would want to still the soul. I think I have always wished for fire from mine."[19] We recall the flammable spirit of *Rhyton*. We recall that fire has so often been a symbol of spirit, as in the flaming tongues of the Holy Spirit. We recall the bricked-up fire of the family. And we recall that the circle or mandala has so often appeared in world cultures as an image of wholeness, of the balance of opposites, and of how things begin and end in a common point. So in this brief exploration of the vision of a single person, Nancy Witt of Virginia, we observe the emergence of archetypal images to incarnate the invisible powers of both personal and archetypal process. As Shakespeare suggested of imagination, this is the power "to lend to airy nothing a local habitation and a name."

Individuating persons contribute their gifts to the collective, and in their private visions, publicly shared, profoundly recharge the most ancient of images. They are all present: earth, air, fire, and water, the four elements of Democritus, the multifoliate rose of Dante, the world's wound healed by beauty which bursts and bestows. And through this vision of a single pair of eyes we are spared Blake's "single vision and Newton's sleep" and are present to the eternal which moves each moment. Such is the gift to us from the artist, the remembrance that, in the words of poet Stephen Dunn, "everything he does takes root, hums / beneath the surfaces of the world."[20]

CHAPTER 4

Therapeutic Imaginings

Psychopathology and Soul

Sunt lacrimae rerum et mentem mortalia tangunt.
These are the tears of things, and the stuff
of our mortality cuts us to the heart.
—Virgil

What we wish most to know, most desire, remains unknowable and lies
beyond our grasp. In a poem titled "Introduction to the 20th Century,"
Stephen Dunn writes,

> *For every*
> *lame god a rhythm and a hunch, something local*
> *we could trust. We learned to put*
> *history books down gently on the table,*
> *conscious of the Hitlers in them, the Stalins,*
> *monsters that were ours and no one else's.*
> *In difficult times, we came to understand,*
> *it's the personal and only the personal that matters.*[1]

I do not know if the poet ever knew that Jung called neurosis a
"wounded god," a telling, hermeneutical metaphor for the depth dynamics of the soul which is repressed, split off, projected. But we all
know the truth of this metaphor, this lame god Dunn evokes in a misshapen century, and in the sundry pathologies of our misshapen lives.

To counter this deep dis-ease, this existential certainty that nothing is any longer certain, we seek our private rhythms, trust the velleities of our intuitions, and rely on the apparently known from which to chart our cautious courses. We know we have bred monsters, and not just in sleep, but in the pasty-faced man with a mustache who gave nightmares to the world, and against which we have to measure all Victorian fantasies of meliorism, progress, and perfectibility. And we know, if we are honest and have ventured out from the quiet porches of our sleeping ancestors, that we carry such monsters within ourselves, that we can no longer point over the distant horizon to dissociate from this hurt, horrible slayer of sleep, reason's renegade, or from the malignities of mind. Dunn, like most modern and postmodern artists, prospects the personal, tracks the truths with small t, and seeks solipsistic solace. With the common ground gone, the metaphysical consensus betrayed, he has little choice. And we have little choice but to continue to link the merely personal with the archetypal, to find what ancient rhythms course within us, even when it is our pathologies which may at last lead us home.

When we recall that the foundation metaphors, or archetypes, represent radical openings to mystery, then we recover the possibility of depth which is missing in modern psychology and psychotherapy. To consciously evoke soul when we practice psychology (the expression of soul) or psychotherapy (the attendance upon soul) or address psychopathology (the suffering of soul) is to recover something original, profound, and generally lost to modern practice. Of course we do not know what soul itself means, but this not knowing is proper to sustain the soul's purchase on mystery. In the etymological metaphors of soul we find both the transmogrifying butterfly and the verb "to breathe," the invisible inspiriting, animating energy which enters the husk of life at birth, undergoes its autonomous permutations, and departs at death.

Tracking this deep, divine breath was historically the task of mythologies, then theologies, and now, when the gods have withdrawn and gone inward as Jung suggests, the task of depth psychology. The lame gods are now psychopathologies and find their incarnation as somatic illness, addictions, sociopathies, neuroses, and personality disorders. Only when we discern the divine dramatic in these patterns will we have any respect for the fact that they are indeed psychodynamic, the dynamics of the soul. Only then can we recall what Jung and Hillman have been saying, only to be more and more ignored, over the course of the twentieth century. Only then can psychopathology be seen not only as the sufferings of the soul but the embodied religious crisis of the modern as well.

I have the greatest of respect for the work of behavioral modification, cognitive therapy, and psychopharmacology, for surely we are repetitive, self-defeating behaviors, the carriers of acquired and unproductive thoughts, and reenactors of our biological lineage. Yet to focus on any of those approaches, at the exclusion of the others, is to fail to engage the whole person. What is needed even more today is a psychotherapy that addresses the wounding to the soul, the healing intentions of the soul, and the developmental motives which emanate from the soul. This psychological attitude restores dignity and depth to our suffering, and to the sacred trust which therapy demands.

Those who work as therapists are frequently obliged to use the ubiquitous *Diagnostic and Statistical Manual* (commonly called the *DSM*). While the purpose of the manual is to facilitate diagnosis, which then presumably assists in the formation of treatment plans, in practice the *DSM* only helps statisticians and insurance companies manage patient care by containing costs. A physician friend of mine recently attended a class given at a prestigious teaching hospital in which he and his colleagues were taught how to identify and treat depression and still have the patient out of the office within ten minutes. One simply asks certain limited questions, inquiring as to sleeping patterns, the presence of irritability, and so on. Then a prescription is written. For the second, and presumably final visit, these same questions are asked. Above all, the teaching physician said to the class, "do not ask any personal questions. Do not ask how their life is going or they will stay beyond ten minutes." I have not made this up. It is the tenor of the times. Indeed, similar anecdotes will be found in the repertoire of anyone practicing therapy today. They represent the reduction of the whole person to a soul-less, fractionated machine. No wonder people distrust the healers nearly as much as the insurance companies.

In the *DSM*, the bible of modern diagnosis for which schools offer full-semester classes on its use, and in modern practice, where those in agencies or those seeking third-party payment are required to employ a diagnostic category, there is no speculation on etiology (which god has been offended), the meaning of this soul's suffering, or the teleological therapeutic which must transpire for healing. Defenders will say that the *DSM* only does what is asked to do, and they are right, but it is itself illustrative of a moral bankruptcy, a failure of nerve before the really important questions. Ludwig Wittgenstein once observed that philosophy is the disease for which it is supposed to be the cure. The *DSM* is a symptom of the bankruptcy of the modern therapeutic imagination and an impediment for which the profession is to blame, the ignorance of which actually adds to the suffering of the individual. I recall one behavioral psychologist who entered analysis with me in New Jersey and who smirked at our first meeting, saying, "Everyone knows when we do our own therapy, we come to a psychodynamic person." That he knew this for himself, and practiced otherwise, is as unconscionable as it is common.

We do not know what the *psyche* is, this noun taken from a verb *psychein*, "to breathe." But therein lies the clue that the psyche is a verb and not a noun, a process and not an entity. To think of the psyche, even the unconscious, as an entity leads to the fallacy of literalism wherein one is more easily seduced by the fantasy of measurement or manipulation, rather than the more respectful effort to track those energies as intentions and to possibly align oneself with them. Jung has noted this difficulty:

> [Our] premises are always far too simple. The psyche is the starting point of all human experience, and all the knowledge we have gained eventually leads back to it. The psyche is the beginning and end of all cognition. It is not only the object of its science, but the subject also. This gives psychology a unique place among all the other sciences: on the one hand there is a constant doubt as to the possibility of its being a science at all, while on the other hand psychology acquires the right to state a theoretical problem the solution of which will be one of the most difficult tasks for a future philosophy.[2]

For psychology to have depth, or even consciousness, it must continue to reflect upon itself, its premises, its assumptions, its self-delusion. We know next to nothing about psyche and even less about the person who comes before us in therapy. How could we know the right course for that person? Perhaps their fate, and their individuation, is a path of suffering, exile, or alienation rather than some state with the smarmy descriptor "well adjusted." As T. S. Eliot once observed, in a world of fugitives, the person going the right direction will appear to be running away. And whatever provisional purchase on reality we attain today will be obviated by psyche's flow tomorrow. Again, the most eloquent voice is that of Jung: "There is a widespread prejudice that analysis is something like a 'cure,' to which one submits for a time and then is discharged healed. That is an . . . error left over from the early days. Analytic treatment could be described as a readjustment of psychological attitude . . . but there is no change which is unconditionally valid over a long period of time."[3]

Jung's emphasis implies not only that there is no fixed view of what is right, and permanent, for a person, but that the psyche's permutations tomorrow will throw today's understanding aside. Moreover, Jung repeatedly emphasized that the therapist has no special knowledge superior to that which the analysand already carries within. The final authority is not, to use a repulsive word, the "shrink," but the emergent testimony of the living psyche. Once again, Jung: "Analysis is not a method . . . of putting things into the patient that were not there before. It is better to renounce any attempt to give direction, and simply to throw into relief everything that the analysis brings to light, so that the patient can see it clearly. . . . Anything he has not acquired himself he will not believe in the long run, and what he takes over from authority merely keeps him infantile. He should rather be put in a position to take his own life in hand."[4]

Surely this respect for the truth which lies within the individual soul, and whose intention is incarnation in the world, has a respectful, even religious character to it. How different such an attitude of participation in the great mystery is from the *DSMs*, from the training of modern psychologists, and from that oxymoronic obscenity, "managed care." The ultimate end of depth psychology is to stand respectfully before inner truth and dare to live it in the world. What blocks each of us is fear—fear of loneliness, fear of rejection, and most of all, fear of largeness. We are all afraid to move from the confining powers of fate into the invitations of our destiny, afraid to step into the largeness of our calling to be who we were meant to be.

Another consideration requires attention here. When Jung says, "a feeling is as indisputable a reality as the existence of an idea,"[5] feeling types will say "of course" and thinking types will learn this truth at their begrudging expense. Jung considered feeling, along with thinking, one of the two rational functions. Sensation and intuition are experiential. But both feeling and thinking weigh, measure, *ratio*, evaluate. So surely, to invoke the popular cliché, to be out of touch with one's feelings is to be separated from a powerful internal guidance mechanism which offers a continuous commentary on the course of our lives and invites behaviors appropriate to those evaluations. But too often we continue to confuse feeling with emotion. Emotion is the raw, neurological discharge of energy when a stimulus occurs. That energy is immediately processed through the screen of the particular person's sensibility, that is, the complexes, culture, and extent of consciousness. What transpires after this screening is feeling, which is fraught not only with judgment but with a content as well. The content of a feeling is not only energy, that is, emotion, but thought as well. That thought may be based on a false premise, a misreading of external reality, but it has its own self-referential character.

Often these thoughts are primitive in character, when they can be rendered conscious. They say something like, "I am afraid of loss," or "I desire safety," or "I wish to hide from this experience," and so on. The more the experience activates the primordial history we all carry, the more primitive, that is, the more unconscious and undifferentiated the thought which is embodied. Thus, even painful feelings are not themselves the pain, but rather embody painful thought and activate the *a priori* belief system which concludes that one is in pain. This is like the man who goes to the physician and says to him, "Doctor, when I touch my head it hurts. When I touch my chest it hurts. When I touch my abdomen it hurts." The doctor gives him a complete examination and says, "I know what your problem is. You have a broken finger."

Confusing emotion with thought and calling it feeling is to be trapped in an unwitting literalism once again. The key to healing lies not only in discernment of thought, with its appropriateness or lack thereof, but also the subjective character of the screen through which the emotional charge has been processed. It is at this point that we come back to the main thread of these discussions, the power of the image to carry energy, value, and even, as a de facto mythology, to dictate behaviors.

As an exemplification of the power of such intrapsychic imagoes, we may examine the way in which they appear in that range of mental and behavioral function which is called the personality disorder. As we know, impaired or distorted mental functioning is generally categorized as psychosis, organic brain syndrome, neurosis, or personality disorder. In the nineteenth century this last category bore a heavy moral freight and included such terms as "moral imbecility" (which had nothing to do with intelligence but was instead concerned with social conformity) or sometimes even "moral insanity." In the twentieth century such individuals were then classified as having "character disorders," still implying some flaw of character, as if a healthy person would automatically and consistently act virtuously. Today, such assumptions appear naive, idiosyncratic, and ethnocentric. (As I was told more than once in Switzerland, a Bavarian, acting like a Bavarian, would in Switzerland be classified as mentally deranged). Personality disorders still create some metaphoric dissonance, and Jungian therapists often refer to "disorders of the Self" instead. This last metaphor, while shunning moralism, comes closer to the truth. While we do not know the Self, that mysterious and dynamic purposefulness in each of us, each of us does have "a sense of Self."

The sense of Self is carried in a congeries of intrapsychic imagoes. Life is inherently traumatic. At birth we are ripped from primordial connection, beneficent belonging, are flung into an uncertain world, and end in annihilation. The magnitude and qualitative character of the inevitable wounding shapes the sensibility of the person, that is, programs the intrapsychic imago in profound and reflexive ways, the imago through which we interpret the spectrum of experiences which come to us. From the child's phenomenological reading of the environment and experiences, a sense of Self, a sense of Other, and acquired strategies of transactions between them are assembled. This assemblage constitutes the inevitable false self or provisional personality with which we enter the world. Invariably it is a misreading, for it lacks alternative experiences, lacks conscious reflectivity, and remains trapped in the fallacy of overgeneralization.

For the child who experiences the world as essentially overwhelming—the abusive father, the needy mother, the grim world of poverty—a profound sense of powerlessness provides the core datum from which a coping strategy must emerge. That person will learn, quite logically in the face of the powerful Other out there, patterns of avoidance, aggression, or most likely, compliance with the demands of the environment. (The more adaptation which is necessitated by environmental demands, the greater the degree of self-alienation.) From such an intrapsychic imago comes, for example, codependence, which always repeats the matrix of the power of the other, to whom one must adapt one's own reality in search of approval of that other.

The child who experiences the world as essentially insufficient, with his or her core needs for nourishment and affirmation unmet, will tend to internalize a sense of self similarly based on absence, will collude with his or her own devaluation, and will enter the world not only with diminished expectations but with self-defeating, confirmative behaviors as well. Or, just as logically, he or she will spend a lifetime soliciting the affirmations of the other. While often choosing persons who are affectively impaired themselves, he or she continues to implore the other for solace, yet expects and usually receives disappointment. From such intrapsychic imagoes, addictive behaviors and replicative relationships transpire.

In that sector of humanity called personality disorders, or disorders of self, we see that the central phenomenon is the power of the intrapsychic imago to overrule the dictates of reason, experience, and the counsel of others. From the outset of modern psychology, therapists recognized a category of patients who could consciously experience their lives but lacked the capacity to reflect, to internalize, gain insight, and to work through toward alternatives. While this dilemma is often found in a wide range of personality disorders, we may here reflect on what has since come to be called the borderline personality disorder. While literature on the phenomenon goes back to the 1890s, the term *borderline* was first used in the 1930s for a group of persons who were not psychotic yet whose conditions did not resemble garden-variety neuroses either.

What is common to all personality disorders, or disorders of self, is that the primordial experiences tend to obliterate the nascent self, which then impairs the developmental capacity of ego to discern conscious alternatives. Most often these primordial experiences are of physical or emotional abuse, sometimes of profound neglect, sometimes from cultural cataclysms but most often from within the family of origin. These primordial experiences fracture the emergent ego and diffuse its core, a process that one may describe as an identity diffusion. Thus, one lacks an integrated sense of self and/or an integrated sense of the other. From this diffuse sense of self one often suffers from feelings of chronic emptiness that are manifest in impoverished relationships with others.

Additionally, the defenses which this person acquires are relatively primitive, as befits the primacy of their etiology. Thus, repression and avoidance are most common, for thereby one escapes the replication of painful, overwhelming experience. Secondly, splitting is common. It is very difficult for this shattered self to handle the stress of anxiety, ambiguity, and ambivalence, so he or she will tend to polarize experiences into all good or all bad. The borderline will enter therapy by exalting the potential embodied by the new therapist, denigrate the former therapist, and turn on the new therapist as soon as he or she fails to meet often unrealistic expectations. So, too, in intimate relationships, the other is all good, but when revealed to be human and flawed, becomes all bad, and one must move quickly to the next person to renew hope.

Because the sense of self is so fragile, he or she cannot hold very much painful affect. Through the mechanism of projective identification, the person projects onto others the painful and intense feelings he or she cannot contain, process, or render conscious. As he or she often fears the intensity of those affects, he or she will implicitly fear the power of the other onto whom such energies have been projected. As a projection is by definition unconscious, one is not aware that the other whom I fear is in fact carrying part of my identity. The stalker is a notable example of a person who is trapped in projective identification, who has projected onto another an essential part of the self and is anxiously needy for that missing piece or terrified of owning it in a personal way. Hence the stalker resists reason, rejection, and even court orders to stay away from the other for he or she is incapable of internalizing. Usually such affairs end in sanctions, incarceration, or the object of projection shifting to someone else, seldom in conscious reflection. Such self-defeating behavior is mute testimony to the power of the intrapsychic imago. What cannot be contained inwardly seemingly must be pursued outwardly. Even more common in borderline behavior is the need to control the other lest those threatening affects have too large an autonomy.

Hand in hand with repression, splitting, and projection goes denial. The borderline personality disorder suffers from an impaired capacity for responsibility, for responsibility requires no small measure of strength and resilience. In order to avoid the problem of painful or inconsistent experiences, the person disowns them by saying, "It is never my fault. You have misunderstood me. You did this or that and caused all of these problems." One could say that the reality of the borderline suffers from excess lability rather than consistency, given that his or her formative experiences no doubt were inconsistent.

Next to nurturance and security, we need consistency in relationships most if we are to form a sense of self which has consistency as well. As a compensation for that inconsistent sense of self, the borderline is often driven to a form of inflation to counterbalance the devalued sense of self. The other plays too large a role in one's life and therefore one is obliged to magnify one's own importance, how misunderstood one is, how much injury has been done to one, or how wonderful one's intentions are.

Most of all, one finds in these personality disorders a resistance to interpretation, that is, to the conscious acknowledgment and affective internalization of the dynamics of his or her life. Developing such a capacity, which is the requisite for growth and change, is often impossible for one with an unstable and fragile sense of self. Even the best efforts of the therapist will be rejected by this hostile rejoinder, which is in fact a sad *cri de coeur*. As one analyst describes it, "'Don't you dare try to find meaning or make sense of this. There is no meaning and there will be none.' This is another way of phrasing the motif of despair: 'My life is bad: Don't you dare see it any other way.'"[6]

It is the recalcitrance of the intrapsychic imago, the fallacy of overgeneralization, which leads to this sad impasse, this repetitive contretemps. The impairment of the ego begets poor impulse control, so that he or she often acts rashly and reaps painful consequences. The ego lacks the capacity to tolerate what Freud calls life's normal miseries, the daily experience of anxiety, ambiguity, and ambivalence. The ego finds little opportunity for sublimation of needs through alternative paths of gratification and instead tends toward obsessional preoccupation with another person, an imagined slight, or a hunger. And he or she often suffers from a poorly developed superego, that is, a set of consistent, normative values, for the value system is most often derivative of obliterating primordial experiences.

We recall Rilke's acknowledgment that the deeper experience of the present beloved was stirred by the memories of the personal mother. But he also knew that the personal mother was a bridge to the realm of the Mothers, that is, to the world of feeling, instinct, body, and world. So, too often, the person who suffers shattering primordial experience not only transfers such dynamics to other relationships, and cannot imagine that these current relationships are possibly unique or different, but has extended the power of the imago to all other relationships as well.

As Rilke evoked the archetypal realm of the mothers, which courses beneath the renewed guise of intimacy and was mediated for good or ill by the primordial encounter with the mother, so the personality disorder is stuck in an archetypal fantasy. The power of the screen which the imago represents, allied with a diminished personal strength, extends the primordial hurt, betrayal, and loss to the universe. While such conclusions are logical, in that they follow a certain primordial sequence, as A was, so B shall be, they also bind one to repetitive history. All of us are wounded. Ordinary neurotics are conscious of their wounds and often conclude that they themselves are their own worst enemy. The personality disorder is subsumed by the wound, identified with it, and can literally imagine no other. He or she is caught in a poverty of imagination. The neurotic tends to take too much responsibility, and the personality disorder, too little. Each suffers, but the former has a greater capacity for growth given that painful measure of responsibility. The neurotic has a greater chance of change from insight, and the personality disorder is best identified by the sad iron wheel of repeated experiences in which he or she, like Ixion of ancient Greece, seems cursed by the gods. While one can learn from the discernment of patterns, the other sees repetition as confirmation, and therefore is predisposed to replication.

Only two therapeutic hopes survive in the treatment of personality disorders. As any therapist will confirm, the therapist is often bullied, manipulated, even vilified by the borderline patient. Therapists tend to burn out and then feel guilty about their anger toward the patient, who consistently resists the therapist's best efforts. Change does occur, sometimes, but only when the intrapsychic imago can be reprogrammed, or better, when an alternative imago of roughly competitive power can be formed. Since insight is seldom internalized, the continued support of the ego, repetition, reinforcement, and support will sometimes provide a reparenting experience. It also allows the formation of, so to speak, an alternative ego derived from another primordial experience. Secondly, in moderate to severe personality disorders, the transference *is* the analysis. That is, the reparenting experience, based on a positive transference, when achievable, is more healing than insight itself. The experience of therapy as the constant context of care creates an alternative to the devastation of earlier experience and can, over time, gestate an enlarged sense of self which makes other choices possible. When one's experience of relationship has caring, affirmation, and constancy, one may be able to make different choices out of an alternative paradigm. Sadly, the power of the first, primordial experience is of such magnitude, that such reparenting, even strongly positive transference, is difficult at best. The paradox of the personality disorder is that the extension of personal, *ad hoc* experience to the archetypal field is illustrative of both the power of the fixated image and the impoverishment of imagination to go beyond it.[7]

The patience and compassion of the therapist are sorely tested by the borderline personality disorder. The therapist is obliged to patiently repeat clarification ("what issue or dynamic is present here?"), confrontation ("why the same response each time?"), and interpretation ("this response comes from what archaic perception?"). And, as Jung always challenged therapists to do, they must present themselves as life models, display a more integrated and variegated response to life's suffering, and show how one can live with courage, dignity, and resilience in a fractious and wounding world.

One illustration may suffice: the story of Marci, a thirty-nine-year-old schoolteacher. Beautiful, intelligent, gifted, energetic, she was forever miserable. Inside her was a poverty, an emptiness, and an obsessive hunger, which were expressed by bouts of bulimia and by hurried, frenetic, reproachful relationships. She had married early, and divorced shortly thereafter, an immature man who made money and used cocaine in ascending order of importance. She had a history of eating disorders, addictions to alcohol and pills, serial relationships, and two suicide attempts. She was the daughter of a narcissistic mother who was neglectful, demanding, and critical and who repeatedly slapped her about. Marci still called her "Mommy." Her father was passive—his job was to make money, take care of Mommy, and keep his mouth shut.

Marci entered therapy in the grip of a new obsessional relationship with Terry, also a passive male still under the thumb of a domineering father. Terry was afraid to alienate his ex-mate by completing a divorce, could not confront his father who continued to control his life, and would not commit to therapy himself. The intrapsychic imago of the primordial experience continues to have its way with both adults. Terry is one of many relationships Marci has had, she having chosen precisely those men who could not be there for her either. Her anger against the immature parents could not be enacted by the child, so the parental imagoes were fueled by a subtext of rage which was enacted by her self-destructive behaviors and her assaults on others. For instance, she telephoned the new girlfriend of her old boyfriend to tell her, falsely, that he was carrying a venereal disease. At the same time Marci is racked by a piteous terror of abandonment. She followed her boyfriends, telephoned them incessantly at work, and generally crowded them out of her life with her incessant need. When asked what she most wished, she replied, "to be adored."

What is necessary to the child, and remained unfulfilled, persists as a primitive, obsessional fantasy for the adult. No one could ever measure up to that need, especially from the crowd of debilitated lovers she had assembled. Both by her choice of partners, and her replicative behaviors, Marci remained chained to the Ixion wheel of repetitive wounding. The therapy transpired over many years and in time evolved toward the introjection of a more stable, constant sense of self, and a more realistic expectation of the other. Her therapy ended with her marriage to the person who followed Terry. One would like to hope that her life is freer than ever before from the power of the past and that the imagination has construed a wider and deeper field in which to play.

Two other, briefer examples of the constriction of the imagination which we call personality disorders may suffice. The sociopathic personality, also known as the antisocial personality, contains its own Janus-faced dilemma. Wounded by society, it wounds society in return. He or she can never replace the possibilities inherent in any new relationship with anything other than the betrayal of the primordial relationships. The antisocial personality's ever-present challenge is, "If mother and father could so betray, how could I ever expect anything different?" Expecting to be wounded ever anew, the sociopath may be overtly aggressive, or silently charming and manipulative, but relationships are always about controlling the other lest one be controlled.

Among the salient characteristics are the following features which emanate from a locked-in imago. A sense of personal entitlement is compensation for generalized feelings of unworthiness and emptiness. The ready exploitation of others derives from fear of others. Why so much fear? Because it is primordial, derived from the powerlessness of the child to defend itself. This historic, reflexive encounter with the other carries a zero-sum conclusion: I use you, or you will surely use me. Antisocial acts represent the sociopath's generalization of all the original destructive dyads to everything and everyone he or she encounters. Transient relationships, multiple marriages, and the inability to commit derive from the fear of bonding with the intimate other, expecting that other will only repeat the world's wounding. An impaired feeling function is ample testimony to a feeling function that was once overwhelmed.

Most of us can bear later traumatizing experiences and not become sociopaths because most people generally have a stronger, more resilient ego, allowing us to base our sense of humanity on more benign paradigms. Demoralizing and devaluing experiences such as imprisonment in a concentration camp could, of course, be sufficiently devastating to one's sense of self and value system as to overwhelm our natural capacity to relate to others, as the powerful novel and film *The Pawnbroker* demonstrated. Lastly, and most importantly, the inability to internalize, to compare and contrast, and to image forth other possibilities is a measure of the magnitude of early devastation of the nascent ego. One sociopath I knew had repeated marriages and was abusive in all of them. The terrible paradox of needing the nurturance of the feminine and at the same time fearing and fighting against it argued for an early traumatic encounter with the mother. Such persons are hard to like, or hard to find empathy for, but inside is a cowering child whose tears would break our heart if we could but hear them. The false self of the sociopath, based on abuse and victimization, buttressed by fear and rage, with its epiphenomenal behaviors of social warfare, is a portrait of terrorizing terror which is itself terrified.

The narcissistic personality disorder is often deceptive to us. Such persons, so vested in control of others, often appear assured and self-possessed, but therein lies their terrible secret. We recall the ancient story of the youth Narcissus, who stares into the pool and falls in love with his own image. We are usually annoyed at narcissists, for we think they are in love with themselves. In fact, their secret is that when they stare into the mirror, no one stares back.

All of us are born with the universal need for identity support, which we acquire through bonding, and mirroring in the faces and behaviors of others. From the "mirror" of others we derive a provisional sense of self, of relative worthiness, and, moreover, an indication of what to expect from the world. When the caregiver is impaired, depressed perhaps, or narcissistic also, little affirming energy flows toward the needy child. He or she then suffers a dramatic deficit, an emotional starvation as it were. He or she will then spend a lifetime seeking solace, seeking love, power, or whatever might fill the terrible emptiness within and persuade others of his or her worth.

Such a person will look to control others, force them to admire him or her. When the narcissist is a parent, the children are used as reflective mirrors to bolster a shaky sense of self. The narcissist in general tries to split relationships among others, to keep them as spokes on a wheel joined to one center. If they talk among themselves, compare notes, and conspire, then the jig is up and they may gather strength to walk away from the needy parent. Because no child can walk away from its own nurturant source, it often takes many years for the mature child to gather strength sufficient to save himself or herself. If a person does attempt to do so, he or she usually endures a great deal of binding guilt, recrimination, and many unsuccessful attempts. If a narcissist can find a dependent personality, as Marci's mother did, then he or she will form a binding relationship but one whose premise is predicated on the defense against emptiness.

We all have narcissistic wounds, inflicted because life is unable to affirm and nurture us when we most need it, but the narcissistic wound is not as systemic as the narcissistic personality disorder, which is defined by that wound. In the more Jungian language of "the disorder of self," the provisional sense of self speaks: "I am he or she who is naught. At mirror's edge I peek timorously, or with bravado, into your eyes to see what stares back at me. I fear always that nothing will return my needy gaze. And my whole life will be a stratagem to move you into a reflective position whereby I might hope to become real."

In the last twenty years of the twentieth century, one heard much about codependence. While it is not yet classified as a personality disorder, it might be characterized as a disorder of self. Codependence has never been included in the *DSM*, but it was seriously debated at the last go-round. Given the ubiquity of codependent behavior, such an inclusion would be a nightmare for insurance companies, for virtually all of us would be candidates.

As is true for personality disorders, codependence is an expression of the problem of power. The world, the adult, and the caregiver have power while the child does not. Power itself is neutral. It is merely the expression of energy between two entities. When caught in a complex, it can be demonic. When the world misuses power, the child is obliged to adapt in profound ways in order to survive. In effect, codependence is an anxiety disorder because the power of the other is implicit in all relationships, having been transferred reflexively from the historic to the contemporary. As one's security lies with the other, so one becomes, reflexively, defined by the other and one is obliged to adapt one's truth to serve the demands of that other. One learns to cover one's actual feelings lest they prove costly in evoking the displeasure of the other. How many individuals do you know who say something painful, and then laugh, as if to mask their pain lest they, fearfully, be taken seriously for having uttered their truth?

Codependents tend to be nervous and uncomfortable when alone. Though they secretly fear others, they have been defined by them and lose a sense of self when the other is not present. They have generally learned to be nice, for niceness is universally adaptive and may sometimes even yield rewards. But to be reflexively nice is to continuously trade one's truth and betray one's integrity, which is not a pretty thing. Many so-called Codependents Anonymous groups are in fact Recovering Nice Persons Anonymous groups.

Codependents routinely place the needs of others before their own. Unlike narcissists, they have learned that to get along you go along, and their own unmet needs are chronic and depressive. To treat this chronic deficit, they are prone to addictions to soften their pain. They are filled with shame, excessively modest, and sabotage their visions. They have learned to keep the peace, usually at all costs. They feel responsible for the well-being of others. And they have difficulties establishing boundaries, the demarcations of legitimate self-interest and self-worth. Many of them grow up to be professional care-givers, such as nurses and social workers, because they have become deeply identified with the power of the other and the diminishment of self. They may be martyrs, or simply always productive persons, but they suffer depression, burnout, and the anguish of the chronically unmet. What we are describing here is a disorder of self, for the integrity of the self is repeatedly and willfully violated in service to the archaic imago.

Roger was the most codependent man I had ever met. For thirty years he was married to a narcissistic woman who, even after their divorce, stalked him, telephoned him in the middle of the night, and sought to control his second marriage. His second wife was understandably distressed when wife number one turned up one day and demanded sex from Roger. Powerless as he was, he consented. Then he was caught in the codependent's nightmare, trying to please competing claims. He knew what he had done was wrong, but he had felt powerless to say no. His therapy involved fundamental reparenting, to give permission and legitimacy to the personal boundaries, and to counter the terrible inequities of power which haunt his primordial imagination.

Healing demands the re-imagining of self and world, and it is not an easy task. The power of the archaic imago accounts for our resistance to change, and thus requires the steady, patient, repetitive work of therapy. We all would like to believe that if we could heal our environment (and some professional caregivers entered their professions in the fantasy that this was possible), then it would be there for us, nurturant, protective, and predictable. If we could fix our partners, get our children to espouse our values, get a better job, acquire more money, or power, or prestige, then life would be better, would it not?

But healing requires that we become psychological, against our will in most cases. Our complexes, our neuroses, our personality disorders all derive from early or especially powerful experience internalized as mythological systems. It is not that we live in a mythless age. We are all in service to those mythological imagoes, those charged value systems, those repetitive world views, which own us and drive us to serve history. We begin to free ourselves from their archaic powers when we can ask, amid the detritus of daily life, these questions: What does this activate in my history? Where does this come from in me? What is the pattern, and its source, which I repeat? What is "the wounded wish" my choices really serve? Such questions are liberating, and to ask them requires strength and courage, for one can no longer blame someone else or seek futilely to invent an external world that will heal us.

Healing is the capacity for reimaging our relationship to the Self. Underneath the sense of self is the Self itself. It is always there, our nature naturing, seeking to become itself, and it is always expressing its holistic intent. The purpose of therapy, whether in company with a therapist or in a dialogue with ourselves, is to attend the teleological voice of the Self when it speaks through the venue of the body, through replicative patterns, through compensatory dream image, through the analysis of complexes, or through the grace of insight and renewing vision.

The source of the self-disorder is not the Self; it is the power of the wounding world. The source of renewal is the still, quiet voice of the Self which may be heard by those who wish to hear, who retain the capacity to hear, or who are driven to hear. As Jung has noted, the encounter with the Self is often experienced as a defeat for the ego. So it is in the experience of defeat that renewal will be found, through a "terrible grace" in which other images may present themselves to consciousness and through the yearning for meaning which leads us through pain to plenitude.

None of us escapes life unscathed, or evades imprisonment by our reactions and misreadings of life's traumata. How difficult, perhaps impossible, to be in the present unless we are in an instinctual response or a re-imagined moment. How powerful is what Freud called the repetition compulsion, not only the reflex but the desire to repeat even wounding history because it is familiar to us. If our friend is our only friend, and that friend repeatedly betrays us, we may still cling to that friend rather than face the terror of a great lonely, unformed freedom. Perhaps the only true pathology is found in denial, for in denial there is no possible purchase on the present. How hard it is to come to responsibility for our lives, to affirm that:

I am responsible for my history (at least after adolescence).
I am responsible for my personal well-being.
I am responsible for my individuation imperative, from which fear alone keeps me separated.

In the category of personality disorders one is trapped in the power of an archetypal imago. For those who remain only neurotic, the identification with one's defenses is natural but regressive. Each of us is presented with a riddle, just as the novice receives in the *koan* of the Zendo: "What you have become is now your problem!" What we have assembled, necessarily, now stands in the way, and we are obliged to risk new attitudes, behaviors, and much larger visions.

Strange as it may seem, we have to invent a "second adulthood" as a necessary fiction, even as the hackneyed "inner child" was invented to acknowledge the power of history. What was too large for that child is now the agenda for the adult. The adult has greater ego strength, capacity for reflection and objectivity, and alternative possibilities unavailable to the child. What restrains us is fear, for sure, and the constraints of the imagination. None of us can escape psycho-pathology, the ubiquitous wounds to the soul, and the distortions of our natural paths which result. The invitation is to summon courage to take on the world anew, to relinquish outmoded identities and defenses, and risk a radical re-imagining of the larger possibilities of the world and of self.

There are lame gods in this world, as Stephen Dunn poetically illustrates, and there are wounded gods at the heart of every soul, as Jung tells us. But the mystery of psyche pulsates and permutates—every time we look in the mirror we are different, and the mirror is different, and wheresoever dying is done, birth is born. As poet Edward Hirsch muses,

> One thinks of the gods dissolving in mid-air
> And the towering stillness of a cathedral at dawn.
> . . . .
> Raindrops break the watery skin of ponds
> And ponds are shattered mirrors of the absolute.[8]

Re-Imagining the Soul

What we wish most to know, most desire, remains unknowable and lies beyond our grasp. Thus, as the meaning-seeking, meaning- creating species, we depend on the image which arises out of depth encounters. This image, as we have seen, is not itself divine, though it carries and is animated by the eternal exchange of that energy which we may call divine. The husk which such energy inhabits is perishable, as we know our own bodies to be. While we would understandably cling to that husk, be it this body, or this ego-concept, or this god, we would be better served trying to hold the ocean in our hands.

The deep stir and tumult has another source, and another end, beyond that which our limited consciousness could ever frame. Yet the fragile reed, as Blaise Pascal reminded us, is a "thinking reed" and courageously conjures with that infinity which could so casually destroy it. That disparity, the longing for eternity and the limits of finitude, is our dilemma, the conscious suffering of which is also what most marks our species. It is the symbolic capacity which defines us uniquely. The images which arise out of the depths, be they the burning bush of biblical imagery, the complaint of the body, or the dream we dream tonight, link us to that throbbing, insistent hum which is the sound of the eternal. As children we listened to the sound of the sea still echoing in the shell we picked up by the shore. That ancestral roar links us to the great sea which surges within us as well.

We perforce recall that psyche and soul have been split in our time, the former assigned to the uneasy calculations of the psychologists, the latter to the rigid fingers of the theologians. Yet, surely, the two are one, for what most deeply affects our relationship to depth, to the gods, permeates our being. The flight of the psychologists from the largeness of this agenda is a form of moral cowardice, and the attempt of much theology to protect us from religious experience is shameful. For both, the reality of the soul is suspect, fearfully avoided, and contributes to the diminution of the spiritual potential of the individual. Who among us has been encouraged to wonder at "the starry skies above and the moral law within," as Kant did? Jung certainly did. In a 1945 letter he writes,

> I know it is exceedingly difficult to write anything definite or descriptive about the progression of psychological states. It always seemed to me as if the real milestones were certain symbolic events characterized by a strong emotional tone. You are quite right, the main interest of my work is not concerned with the treatment of neuroses but rather with the approach to the numinous. But the fact that the approach to the numinous is the real therapy and inasmuch as you attain to the numinous experiences you are released from the curse of pathology. Even the very disease takes on a numinous character.[1]

Even the disease takes on a numinous character! You will not find that sentence in the *DSM-IV,* and that is what is wrong with modern psychology—it has no soul, that is, no depth, and is unintentionally demeaning to the person and his or her own high calling. Moreover, as Jung says, the approach to the numinous is the real therapy. Thus any therapist, any cleric who does not suffer and persist in a personal engagement with the problem of meaning, with the forever transforming numinous, cannot be said to be part of a healing or enlarging process.

While describing and counting behaviors may be provisionally useful and certainly contribute to statistics, such an approach to psychology may prove an unwitting contrivance to avoid the numinous. One recalls the wry observation of Benjamin Disraeli who said that there are three kinds of lies: lies, damn lies, and statistics. It is for this reason that Jungian psychology has sought its grounding in myth, the *Märchen,* alchemical texts, and other suspect sources. As Richard Tarnas observes, the transcendent may be "approached through myth and the poetic imagination, as well as by attending to a kind of aesthetic resonance within the psyche touched off by the presence of the archetypal in veiled form with the phenomenal world."[2]

The release from pathology is by numinous encounter, which may shatter the ego states but which brings one into enlarged experience. This movement of psyche is best discerned in the creative act of myth, dream, and fantasy. The limits of our condition were well expressed by Protagoras twenty-five hundred years ago: "Concerning the gods, I have no means of knowing whether they exist or not, nor of what form they are; for there are many obstacles to such knowledge, including the obscurity of the subject and the shortness of human life."[3]

Our dilemma is even more dramatically described by the Thai Buddhist monk Ajahn Chah:

> Nowhere in the world is there any real peace to be found. The poor have no peace and neither do the rich. Adults have no peace, children have no peace, the poorly educated have no peace, and neither do the highly educated. There is no peace anywhere. That is the nature of the world.
>
> Those who have few possessions suffer and so do those who have many. Children, adults, the aged, everyone suffers. The suffering of being old, the suffering of being young, the suffering of being wealthy, and the suffering of being poor—it's all nothing but suffering. . . . Every single moment we are undergoing birth and death. That is the way things are.[4]

Yet all around are what Wordsworth called intimations of immortality—intimations, not certainties, but nonetheless real. When Jesus said that his kingdom was spread all over the earth and we did not see it, and Paul Éluard asserted that the other world, the invisible world, is this one, then, in the midst of finitude, death, and suffering, there is still something which beckons, something which summons us to enlarged vocation. Jung defines the imperative of individuation as a vocation. It is, he says, "an irrational factor which destines a man to emancipate himself from the herd and from its well-worn paths. True personality is always a vocation and puts its trust in it as in God . . . but vocation acts like a law of God from which there is no escape."[5]

What summons us forth, then, is the image which is not the divine but for the moment contains the numinous. We recall that for Jung, the archetypal shaping process is not only the work of instinct, though it is surely that to some extent, but also the shaping of energy into images which have spiritual import. Such images arise autonomously out of depth experience and may be found in the cataclysmic *metanoia* of Saul on the road to Damascus, in the metarealistic topography of dreamscapes, or in the lowliest of creatures, as we remember the humble dung beetle, scarab of the sacred. For us to re-collect the soul, to re-member psyche, we are enjoined to the contemplation of the poet rather than the pathologist and the artist rather than the psychologist.

Poet Stephen Dunn summons such an encounter with the transcendent through the image of the lowliest of creatures, the common fly, in a poem titled "The Resurrection."

The poet has been sitting, waiting for the uncertain muse to make its appearance on a winter's day. Nothing . . . his eye catches a fly whose somnolence has been stirred by the warming room and which now begins to stir and flit about. Something within the poet also stirs at this simplest of events; the archetypal imagination is activated toward a dramaturgy deeper than the mundane character of the object itself. It tumbles over the banal into the divine; it is

> *a phenomenon that could turn a boy*
> *from street crime to science*
> *or, if less bright, to the church.*

He is captured by the fly relearning flight, pushing against the window, with its little fly's heart. His blood stirred by some ancient tremor, some archetypal ceremony, Dunn decides that he has been summoned to be the poet of this fly, for all things great and small surely deserve a witness to their troubled transit.

As a conscious being, Dunn knows what the fly cannot yet know, that the room is finite, that the respite is fleeting, and that cold death still waits beyond the warm room. And the archetypal analogues are inescapable. We, the most fleeting, as Rilke reminded us, like the fly rise from torpor and fling ourselves against the transparent limits of desire.

To be a fly
was to fly in the face
of all that could defeat it,
and there was the pleasure of shit
to look forward to, the pleasure of bothering
cows and people, the pleasure of pure speed.

Being here, we, too, are the most transient of beings, humming and buzzing from shit to aesthetics. Then the poet sees other flies rise and dash about madly. He concludes that, for now at least, he has been summoned to be the

. . . poet of flies in winter
as they sought the other side
of the glass, which was death,
victims of having once risen, ignorant
buggers, happy on bad evidence, warm, abuzz.[6]

We, ignorant buggers, happy on bad evidence, warm, abuzz for now, are stirred by the lowliest creatures, for in their story the gods are passing and the deepest drama of which we too are a passing part. On the other side of the transparent windows lies cold death, but for now there is only the joy of this furious buzzing we call life. Each of our neuroses is wrapped around this paradox, as a defense against it, an ignorant protest, or a secret collusion.

How could we be lifted from our pathologies, Jung asked, if we are not imaginatively open to the depth of those energies which both conflate us and tumble us in harness to the sea? The approach to the numinous, he insisted, is the true therapy. It will no more spare us suffering or death than the other buzzing buggers which have been a moment on this earth. But, by way of the archetypal imagination, these buzzing buggers of which we are a part have intimations of immortality, are participants in a recurrent eschatological drama, and bring their small individuated piece to the great mosaic.

What we wish most to know, most desire, remains unknowable and lies beyond our grasp. The sea changes of the soul are swift and sure and the powers of darkness many, but the gods still speak through the natural forms, through the mysterious dream-maker, and through the archetypal imagination. Our hope and task should be that we might humbly learn to petition the gods again, as in the short supplication of a "Stone from Delphi," by the Nobel Prize–winning poet Seamus Heaney:

> *To be carried back to the shrine some dawn*
> *when the sea spreads its far sun-crops to the south*
> *and I make a morning offering again:*
> that I may escape the miasma of spilled blood,
> govern the tongue, fear hybris, fear the god
> until he speaks in my untrammeled mouth.[7]

Notes

Foreword

1. Anthony Storr, *Solitude: A Return to the Self* (New York: Ballantine Books, 1988).
2. Joan Chodorow, Introduction to C. G. Jung, *Jung on Active Imagination* (Princeton, N.J.: Princeton University Press, 1997), p. 1.
3. Ibid., pp. 2–20.
4. See Verena Kast, *Joy, Inspiration, and Hope* (College Station: Texas A&M University Press, 1991); Thomas Moore, *Care of the Soul* (New York: HarperCollins, 1992); James Hillman, *The Soul's Code: In Search of Character and Calling* (New York: Warner Books, 1997); Mihaly Csikszentmihalyi, *Flow: The Psychology of Optimal Experience* (New York: HarperPerennial, 1990); David H. Rosen and Michael C. Luebbert, eds., *Evolution of the Psyche* (Westport, Conn.: Praeger Publishers, 1999); and Anthony Stevens and John Price, *Evolutionary Psychiatry: A New Beginning* (New York and London: Routledge, 1996).
5. Alice Walker, *The Same River Twice: Honoring the Difficult* (New York: Scribner, 1996), p. 13.

Introduction. Archetypal Imaginings: The Golden String Which Leads to Heaven's Gate

1. Thomas Nashe, "A Litany in the Time of Plague," in *The Norton Anthology of Poetry*, 3rd ed., ed. Alexander Allison et al. (New York: Norton, 1983), p. 202.
2. For a relatively modern example of Jung being identified with Lamarckism, see Henri F. Ellenberger, *The Discovery of the Unconscious* (New York: Basic Books, 1970), pp. 760ff.

3. William Blake, letter to Rev. Dr. Trusler, in *The Poetry and Prose of William Blake*, ed. David V. Erdman (Garden City, N.Y.: Doubleday, 1965), p. 677.

4. Blake, "Letter to Thomas Butts," in *The Poetry and Prose of William Blake*, p. 693.

5. Blake, "The Laocoon," in *The Poetry and Prose of William Blake*, p. 271.

6. This exchange took place during Huston Smith's presentation at a conference titled "Reflections of the Spirit," held at the University of Houston, Honors College, September, 1998.

7. William Wordsworth, "Lines: Composed a Few Miles above Tintern Abbey," in *The Norton Anthology of Poetry*, p. 525.

8. Blake, "Jerusalem," in *The Poetry and Prose of William Blake*, p. 229.

Chapter 1. Religious Imaginings: Divine Morphologies

1. Edward Hirsch, "At the Grave of Wallace Stevens," in *Earthly Measures: Poems* (New York: Alfred A. Knopf, 1994), p. 80.

2. Robert Frost, "Desert Places," in *Modern Poems: An Introduction to Poetry*, ed. Richard Ellmann and Robert O'Clair (New York: Norton, 1976), p. 80.

3. Zora Neale Hurston, *Their Eyes Were Watching God* (1937; reprint, New York: Harper and Row, 1990), p. 183.

4. C. G. Jung, *Letters* (Princeton, N.J.: Princeton University Press, 1973), 2:569.

5. See C. G. Jung, *Alchemical Studies*, in *The Collected Works*, ed. F. C. Hull (Princeton, N.J.: Princeton University Press, 1973), 13:37 (hereafter cited by individual title with *CW* volume and page number).

6. T. S. Eliot, "The Hollow Man," in *T. S. Eliot: The Complete Poems and Plays* (New York: Harcourt, Brace, and World, 1962), p. 58.

7. C. G. Jung, *Memories, Dreams, Reflections*, ed. Aniela Jaffe (New York: Pantheon Books, 1963), p. 340.

8. Dante Alighieri, *The Comedy of Dante Alighieri*, trans. Dorothy Sayers (New York: Basic Books, 1962), p. 347.

9. See Jung, *Psychological Types, CW* 6:480.

10. See, e.g., Jung, *Psychology and Religion: East and West, CW* 11:330.

11. Jung, *The Archetypes and the Collective Unconscious, CW* 9:63.

12. Jung, *Memories, Dreams, Reflections*, p. 340.

13. Jung, *Aion, CW* 9:180.

14. Eliot, "The Hollow Men," p. 212.
15. Jung, *Symbols of Transformation, CW* 5:308.
16. Jung, *The Symbolic Life, CW* 18:275.
17. Jung, *Archetypes and the Collective Unconscious, CW* 9:14–15.
18. From the gnostic sayings of Jesus as cited by Joseph Campbell in *The Masks of God: Occidental Mythology* (New York: Penguin Books, 1976), p. 364.
19. Carl Kerenyi, *Zeus and Hera: Archetypal Image of Father, Husband, and Wife* (Princeton, N.J.: Princeton University Press, 1975), p. xiii.
20. Gerard Manley Hopkins, "Pied Beauty," in *The Norton Anthology of Poetry,* p. 876.
21. Kerenyi, *Zeus and Hera,* p. 5.
22. Jung, *Letters,* 2:525.
23. Wallace Stevens, "Sunday Morning," in *The Norton Anthology of Poetry,* p. 931.
24. Jung, *Archetypes and the Collected Unconscious, CW* 9:6.
25. Ibid.
26. Ibid., p. 7.
27. Kerenyi, *Zeus and Hera,* p. xiv.
28. I am indebted for some of this information to Jungian therapist Ronnie Landau of Philadelphia.
29. James George Frazer, *The Golden Bough: A Study in Magic and Religion* (New York: Macmillan, 1951), p. 3.
30. Jung, *Psychological Types, CW* 6:480.

Chapter 2. Literary Imaginings: Envisioned Logos

1. Kerenyi, *Zeus and Hera,* p. xiv.
2. Rainer Maria Rilke, *Ahead of All Parting: The Selected Poetry and Prose of Rainer Maria Rilke,* trans. Stephen Mitchell (New York: Modern Library, 1995), p. 550.
3. Søren Kierkegaard, *Either/Or,* trans. Walter Lowrie (Princeton, N.J.: Princeton University Press, 1944), 1:15.
4. Unless otherwise noted, this and subsequent quotations are from Rilke's "Third Elegy" and are translated by the author.
5. Quoted in Brenda Maddox, *Nora: The Real Life of Molly Bloom* (Boston, Mass.: Houghton Mifflin, 1988), p. 301.

6. Jonathan Edwards, *Selected Writings of Jonathan Edwards*, ed. Harold Simonson (New York: Waveland Press, 1992), p. 103.

7. Jung, *Symbols of Transformation, CW* 5:355–56.

8. W. B. Yeats, "Nineteen Hundred and Nineteen," in *Selected Poems and Two Plays of William Butler Yeats*, ed. M. L. Rosenthal (New York: Macmillan, 1962), p. 109.

9. Dylan Thomas, "Fern Hill," in *The Norton Anthology of Poetry*, p. 1181.

10. Unless otherwise noted, this and subsequent quotations are from Rilke's "Ninth Elegy" and are translated by the author.

11. Jung's *Answer to Job* is found in *Psychology and Religion*, vol. 11 of *The Collected Works*.

12. Cited by Mitchell in Rilke, *Ahead of All Parting*, p. 568.

13. Archibald MacLeish, "Not Marble Nor Gilded Monuments," in *Poems, 1924–1933* (Boston and New York: Houghton Mifflin, 1933), p. 48.

14. Jung, *Memories, Dreams, Reflections*, p. 326.

15. Cited by Mitchell in Rilke, *Ahead of All Parting*, pp. 569–70.

16. I take part of the title of this section from an essay, "On the Naming of the Gods in Hölderlin and Rilke," written by my graduate advisor and mentor Stanley Romaine Hopper, dean of the Graduate School of Drew University. I offer this chapter in honor of his great teaching.

17. Friedrich Hölderlin, "Patmos," my translation.

18. St. Augustine, *Confessions* (Washington, D.C.: Catholic University Press, 1967), p. 34.

19. Martin Heidegger, "Hölderlin and the Essence of Poetry," in *Existence and Being* (London: Vision Press, 1949), p. 312.

20. Jung, *Psychological Types, CW* 6:190.

21. Rilke, "I Find You in All Things," author's translation.

22. Rilke, "Lament," in Angel Flores, trans., *An Anthology of German Poetry from Hölderlin to Rilke in English Translation* (Garden City, N.Y.: Anchor Books, 1960), p. 386.

23. Ibid.

24. Rilke, "Autumn," in Flores, trans., *An Anthology of German Poetry*, p. 390.

25. Rilke, "Now is the time when the Gods emerge," author's translation.

26. Ibid.

27. Jung, *Archetypes and the Collective Unconscious, CW* 9:62; *Mysterium Coniunctionis, CW* 14:546.

28. Rilke, "Now is the time when the Gods emerge."

29. Ibid.

30. Yeats, "Two Songs from a Play," in *The Norton Anthology of Poetry,* p. 114.

Chapter 3. Incarnational Imaginings: The Painter's Eye on Eternity

1. James Hillman, *The Dream and the Underworld* (New York: Harper and Row, 1979), p. 27.

2. James Hillman, *Re-Visioning Psychology* (New York: Harper and Row, 1975), p. 169.

3. Ibid., p. 154.

4. Jung, *The Spirit in Man, Art, and Literature, CW* 15:101.

5. Rilke, "Love Song," in Flores, trans., *An Anthology of German Poetry,* p. 391.

6. Nancy Witt, *On Alternate Days* (Ashland, Va.: Cross Mill Gallery, 1995), p. 6.

7. Nancy Witt, personal communication with the author.

8. Ibid.

9. Jung, "The Psychological Foundation for the Belief in Spirits," in *The Structure and Dynamics of the Psyche, CW* 8:301.

10. Ibid., p. 304.

11. Ibid., p. 309.

12. Ibid., p. 315.

13. Witt, personal communication.

14. Ibid.

15. Wallace Stevens, "A High-toned Old Christian Woman," in *Modern Poems,* ed. Ellmann and O'Clair, p. 90.

16. Witt, *On Alternate Days,* p. 29.

17. Jung, *The Symbolic Life, CW* 18:451.

18. Gerard Manley Hopkins, "The Windhover," in *A Hopkins Reader* (New York: Anchor-Doubleday, 1966), p. 50.

19. Witt, *On Alternate Days,* p. 81.

20. Stephen Dunn, "The Guardian Angel," in *New and Selected Poems: 1974–1994* (New York: Norton, 1994), p. 204.

Chapter 4. Therapeutic Imaginings: Psychopathology and Soul

1. Dunn, "Introduction to the 20th Century," in *New and Selected Poems: 1974–1994*, p. 83.
2. Jung, *The Structure and Dynamics of the Psyche*, CW 8:125.
3. Ibid., p. 23.
4. Jung, *Freud and Psychoanalysis*, CW 4:278.
5. Jung, *The Practice of Psychotherapy*, CW 16:313.
6. Nathan Schwartz-Salant, *The Borderline Personality: Vision and Healing* (Wilmette, Ill.: Chiron Publications, 1989), p. 29.
7. Such impoverishment of the imagination is the source of racism and bigotry, for the bigot cannot imagine any variant from the stereotype he or she carries. To imagine the pain of the other (sym-pathy) is to experience once's own humanity in the other.
8. Hirsch, "At the Grave of Wallace Stevens," in *Earthly Measures*, p. 80.

Afterword. Re-Imagining the Soul

1. Immanual Kant, *Critique of Practical Reason* (New York: Macmillan, 1992), p. 84; Jung, *Letters*, 1:377.
2. Richard Tarnas, *The Passion of the Western Mind: Understanding the Ideas That Have Shaped Our World View* (New York: Ballantine Books, 1991), p. 54.
3. Cited in ibid., p. 28.
4. Ajahn Chah, "Our Real Home," in *Entering the Stream: An Introduction to the Buddha and His Teachings*, ed. Samuel Bercholz and Sherab Chodzin Kohn (Boston: Shambhala Publications, 1993), pp. 95–96.
5. Jung, *The Development of Personality*, CW 17:175–76.
6. Stephen Dunn, "The Resurrection," in *New and Selected Poems: 1974–1994*, p. 31.
7. Seamus Heaney, "Stone from Delphi," in *Opened Ground: Selected Poems, 1966–1996* (New York: Farrar, Straus and Giroux, 1998), p. 207.

Bibliography

Blake, William. *The Poetry and Prose of William Blake.* Edited by David V. Erdman. Garden City, N.Y.: Doubleday, 1965.

Chah, Ajahn. "Our Real Home." In *Entering the Stream: An Introduction to the Buddha and His Teachings.* Edited by Samuel Bercholz and Sherab Chodzin Kohn. Boston: Shambhala Publications, 1993.

Chodorow, Joan. Introduction to C. G. Jung, *Jung on Active Imagination..* Princeton, N.J.: Princeton University Press, 1997.

Csikszentmihalyi, Mihaly. *Flow: The Psychology of Optimal Experience.* New York: HarperPerennial, 1990.

Diagnostic Criteria from DSM-IV. Washington, D.C.: American Psychiatric Association, 1994.

Dunn, Stephen. *New and Selected Poems: 1974–1994.* New York: Norton, 1994.

Eliot, T. S. *T. S. Eliot: The Complete Poems and Plays.* New York: Harcourt, Brace, and World, 1962.

Flores, Angel, trans. *An Anthology of German Poetry from Hölderlin to Rilke.* Garden City, N.Y.: Anchor Books, 1960.

Frazer, James George. *The Golden Bough: A Study in Magic and Religion.* New York: Macmillan, 1951.

Heidegger, Martin. *Existence and Being.* London: Vision Press, 1949.

Hillman, James. *The Dream and the Underworld.* New York: Harper and Row, 1979.

———. *Re-Visioning Psychology.* New York: Harper and Row, 1975.

———. *The Soul's Code: In Search of Character and Calling.* New York: Warner Books, 1997.

Hirsch, Edward. *Earthly Measures: Poems.* New York: Alfred A. Knopf, 1994.

Jung, Carl Gustav. *The Collected Works.* 20 vols. Edited by F. C. Hull. Princeton, N.J.: Princeton University Press, 1973.

———. *Letters.* 2 vols. Princeton, N.J.: Princeton University Press, 1973.

————. *Memories, Dreams, Reflections.* Edited by Aniela Jaffe. New York: Pantheon Books, 1963.

Kant, Immanuel. *Critique of Practical Reason.* New York: Macmillan, 1992.

Kast, Verena. *Joy, Inspiration, and Hope.* College Station: Texas A&M University Press, 1991.

Kerenyi, Carl. *Zeus and Hera: Archetypal Image of Father, Husband, and Wife.* Princeton, N.J.: Princeton University Press, 1975.

Kierkegaard, Søren. *Either/Or, Volume 1.* Translated by Walter Lowrie. Princeton, N.J.: Princeton University Press, 1944.

Moore, Thomas. *Care of the Soul.* New York: HarperCollins, 1992.

Rilke, Rainer Maria. *Ahead of All Parting: The Selected Poetry and Prose of Rainer Maria Rilke.* Translated by Stephen Mitchell. New York: Modern Library, 1995.

Rosen, David H., and Michael C. Luebbert, eds. *Evolution of the Psyche.* Westport, Conn.: Praeger Publishers, 1999.

Schwartz-Salant, Nathan. *The Borderline Personality: Vision and Healing.* Wilmette, Ill.: Chiron Publications, 1989.

Stevens, Anthony, and John Price. *Evolutionary Psychiatry: A New Beginning.* New York and London: Routledge, 1996.

Storr, Anthony. *Solitude: A Return to the Self.* New York: Ballantine Books, 1988.

Tarnas, Richard. *The Passion of the Western Mind: Understanding the Ideas That Have Shaped Our World View.* New York: Ballantine Books, 1991.

Witt, Nancy. *On Alternate Days.* Ashland, Va.: Cross Mill Gallery, 1995.

Index

religion: etymology of, 22; greatest ideas of, 30; modern context of, 54; psychological dimension of, 24; subjective confession of, 86

Rilke, Rainer Maria, xii, 6, 67, 79, 127; biography of, 35; themes of, 35

St. Augustine, 54, 128

Schliemann, Heinrich, 30

Schwartz-Salant, Nathan, 130n 6

Shakespeare, William, 39, 49, 98

Smith, Huston, 7, 126n 6

speech, constituent power of, 6, 49, 51, 54

spiritual malaise, 75, 100, 101, 120

Stanford University, 9

Stevens, Wallace, 22, 88, 89, 127n 23, 129n 15

Storr, Anthony, xi, 125n 1

symbol, 4, 7, 12, 13, 16, 25, 26, 34, 48, 54, 60, 73, 90, 119

Symbols of Transformation (Jung), 32

Taoism, xi

Taos Pueblo, 15

Tarnas, Richard, 120, 121, 130n 2

Thales, 20

Theosophical Society, 31

Thomas, Dylan, 28, 47, 128n 9

Tillich, Paul, 30

Vaihinger, Hans, 10

Wagner, Richard, 37, 52

Walker, Alice, xiii, 125n 5

Whitehead, Alfred North, 21

Whitman, Walt, 41

Witt, Nancy: "Bailey Won," 91–94; biography of, 62, 63, 64, 65, 71, 78, 91, 97; "Capron," 71–76; "Chalice," 80; "Cicatrice," 94–96; "Glass Darkly," 88–90; "Inside," 68–71; metarealism of, 63, 64; "Opening," 65–68; "Painting," 90; "Rhyton," 86–88; "Ring of Fire," 96–98; "Second Opening," 84–86; "Sue's Fan," 76–80; "Windows," 80–83

Wordsworth, William, 7, 8, 126n 7

Yeats, William Butler, 43, 58, 128n 8, 129n 3

Carolyn and Ernest Fay Series in Analytical Psychology
David H. Rosen, General Editor
TEXAS A&M UNIVERSITY PRESS